A Practical Guide
to Child and Youth Care

Heather Stewart
Richard Nash

Library and Archives Canada Cataloguing in Publication

Stewart, Heather; Nash, Richard
    A practical guide to child and youth care / Heather Stewart and Richard Nash.

978-1-897160-94-7

1. Effective teaching--Handbooks, manuals, etc.
2. Learning strategies--Handbooks, manuals, etc. I. Title.

Copyright © 2021 de Sitter Publications

All rights are reserved. No part of this publication may be reproduced, translated, stored in a retrieval system or transmitted in any form or by any means, electronic, mechanical, photocopying, recording or otherwise, without prior written permission from the publisher.

Cover design by de Sitter Publications
Cover image and content pictures are licensed Abobe Stock
Content design and layout by de Sitter Publications

de Sitter Publications
111 Bell Dr., Whitby, ON, L1N 2T1
CANADA

deSitterPublications.com
289-987-0656
info@desitterpublications.com

Contents

Introduction   1

    Organization of the Textbook   1
    Acknowledgements   3
    About the Authors   3

Chapter 1: What is Child and Youth Care?   5

    Real Life Story   5
    Definition of a CYC Practitioner   5
    Statistics 4212 - Community and SSW   7
    History of CYC   9
    Scope of Practice   10
    Personal Qualities   14
    Employability Skills   17
    Let's Reflect   20
    Worksheet   21
    Checklist   21
    References and Resources   22

Chapter 2: What are CYC Competencies?   23

    Real Life Story   23
    Domains of Practice for Child and Youth Work   23
    Professionalism   24
    Cultural and Human Diversity   27
    Applied Human Development   29
    Relationships & Communication   31
    Developmental Practice Methods   35
    Let's Reflect   42
    Worksheet   43
    Checklist   44
    References and Resources   45

Chapter 3: How Does the Code of Ethics Apply to CYC Practice? 47

Real Life Story 47

Ethnics of CYC Professionals 48

Let's Reflect 52

Worksheet 53

Checklist 54

References and Resources 55

Chapter 4: What is the CYFSA and the YCJA and How Does it Impact my Work? 57

Real Life Story 57

Overview of the CYFSA 57

Overview of Youth Criminal Justice Act 70

Let's Reflect 79

Worksheet 80

Checklist 81

References and Resources 81

Chapter 5: What Does a CYC Do and Where Do They Do It? 85

Real Life Story 85

Introduction 85

Social and Community Service Workers 87

School-Based Setting 90

Hospital Setting 90

Residential/Group Home Setting 91

Child Welfare Setting 92

Let's Reflect 93

Worksheet 94

Checklist 95

References and Resources 95

Chapter 6: What is Abuse and How Does it Impact Children and Adolescents?   97

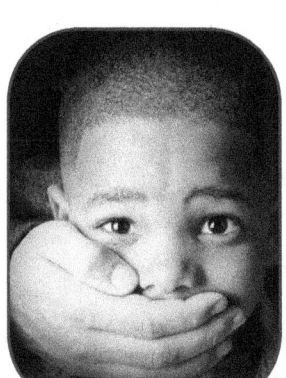

Real Life Story   97

Introduction   98

Physical Abuse   99

Sexual Abuse   99

Neglect   100

Real Life Story   101

Real Life Story   102

Emotional Abuse   102

Exposure to Family Violence   103

Real Life Story   103

Real Life Story   104

Canadian Statistics   105

Let's Reflect   106

Worksheet   107

Checklist   108

References and Resources   108

Chapter 7: What is a Therapeutic Relationship and How Do I Create Professional Boundaries?   109

Real Life Story   109

Therapeutic Relationship   109

Trust   111

Respect   112

Power   112

Professional Boundaries   113

The Professional Relationship Continuum   113

Katelynn's Principle   117

Let's Reflect   118

Worksheet   119

Checklist   120

References and Resources   120

Chapter 8: What is Evidence-Based Practice and Treatment Models   121

Real Life Story   109
What is Evidence-Based Practice?   122
What is Life Space Intervention?   122
10 Evidence-Based Treatment Models   123
Let's Reflect   128
Worksheet   131
Checklist   131
References and Resources   132

Chapter 9: Why Include Family and Significant Others in the Planning for Children and Youth?   133

Real Life Story   133
The Importance of Family   133
Maintaining Family Relationships   134
Kin/Kith Options   134
What is Kinship Service?   135
What is Kinship Care?   135
What is Customary Care in Ontario   136
Supporting Cultural Heritage   137
Signs of Safety   139
Let's Reflect   141
Worksheet   142
Checklist   142
References and Resources   143

Chapter 10: How to Engage Families in Your Practice   145

Real Life Story   145
CYC Approach to Family Work   145
Who is Your Client?   145
Parenting support   150
Parenting Education Programs   151
Let's Reflect   152
Worksheet   153
Checklist   153
References and Resources   154

Chapter 11: What are Burnout and Vicarious Trauma and How Do I Manage Them? 155

Real Life Story   155
Burnout   156
Vicarious Trauma   156
Risk Factors   157
Reducing Risk   159
Organizational Protective Factors   160
Self Reflection   160
Reflective Supervision   161
Reflections ON Action   162
Reflections iN Action   162
Reflections FOR Action   163
Let's Reflect   165
Worksheet   166
Checklist   167
References and Resources   168

Chapter 12: How do I Balance Education, Work and Personal Life? 169

Real Life Story   169
Education   170
Work   171
The Difference Between Stress and Burnout   172
Self Care   172
Let's Reflect   176
Worksheet   177
Checklist   178
References and Resources   178

Introduction

This book is the culmination of our 50+ years of experience as front line workers in various milieus with children, youth, their families, and community partners. Our desire is to provide Child and Youth Care students and practitioners with a resource that is up-to-date and contains real life examples from the field.

In today's times, more than ever, children, youth and their families are struggling to maintain a family unit that is cohesive, positive and risk free. We wrote this guidebook during the Covid 19 pandemic. This brought to life the real struggles of families, youth and children.

During this time children did not have the respite of school and parents were faced with additional challenges of online education and extra care. Parents had little personal time to deal with issues and concerns. This was a grave time for anyone involved in any area of child welfare and for individuals working in the field of Child and Youth Care.

Anyone working during these times recognizes these struggles and the increased risk to our children and youth. This textbook provides a practical guide to support workers and students through their educational and practical journey.

This textbook reflects an up-to-date rendition of the CYFSA and the YCJA, which are pivotal to our work in the field and provides us with guidelines within which we practice.

Organization of the Textbook

This text consists of 12 chapters that best reflected the needs of students and Child and Youth Care practitioners.

Each chapter includes the following special features:

A real-life story: The stories are all true and are examples of personal experiences we encountered, and continue to encounter, during our CYC practice.

Let's Reflect: Much of the CYC field is driven by reflection to allow practitioners to grow and understand their work and thought processes. This section provides a guided reflection based on reflective questions relevant to the chapter content.

Worksheet: The worksheets allow students to test their understanding of the terms, concepts, and objectives of each chapter. The worksheets can also be used as a resource for teachers.

Checklist: Each chapter ends with a checklist to further reinforce the reader's learning and skill development. This can also be a useful resource for teachers, practicum advisors, and placement supervisors.

Chapter 1: What is Child and Youth Care?

This chapter introduces the reader to the field of Child and Youth Care. It includes a brief review of the history, current state, and views on the future of the field.

Chapter 2: What are the Child and Youth Care Competencies?

This chapter explores the Child and Youth Care competencies which are the core values and practice models for effective, accountable, and informed practice within the field.

Chapter 3: How does the Code of Ethics Apply to CYC Practice?

This chapter introduces the reader to the CYC code of ethics, the guidelines and moral rules that guide our practice.

Chapter 4: What is the CYFSA and the YCJA and How Do They Impact my Work?

This chapter introduces the new CYFSA; Child Youth and Family Services Act (which replaced the CFSA in 2018). This is an up-to-date rendition of the current legislation and how it relates to Child and Youth Care Practice. The YCJA also is presented in its most recent publication and applies its principles to CYC practice.

Chapter 5: What Does A CYC Do and Where Do They Do It?

In this chapter we discuss the various environments in which a CYC may find employment and what the requirements and job duties might include for each milieu.

Chapter 6: What is Abuse and How Does it Impact Children and Adolescents?

In this chapter the reader will learn about the different kinds of abuse, how to identify the signs and symptoms, and how to support children, youth and families.

Chapter 7: What is A Therapeutic Relationship and How Do I Create Professional Boundaries?

This chapter defines the meaning of a therapeutic relationship and what that looks like in terms of their practice and interaction with children, youth and families.

Chapter 8: What is Evidence-Based Practice and Treatment Models?

This chapter will take the reader through several "tried and true" methodologies and strategies to incorporate in their practice.

Chapter 9: Why Include Family and Significant Others in Planning For Children and Youth?

This chapter takes the reader through the process of involving family in the context of Child and Youth Care practice. It discusses safe, viable and realistic options for children and youth along with methods for decision making in the best interest of the child.

Chapter 10: How to Engage Families in Your Practice?

In this chapter the reader will learn methods, strategies and reasons to include and engage family's in their work.

Chapter 11: What are Vicarious Trauma and Burnout and How Do I Manage Them?

This chapter explores and defines the signs, symptoms and risks of burnout and vicarious trauma and presents self care methods to assist with the possible outcomes.

Chapter 12: How Do I Balance Education, Work and Personal Life?

In this chapter readers will learn tips and tricks to manage multiple responsibilities while maintaining positive outcomes and participating in self care.

Acknowledgements

We would be remiss if we did not acknowledge our families, their support, patience and understanding while we navigated this process.

Thank you to Stephanie and Eric for understanding our Coffee Culture dates, the Penski file, and the ongoing texts and phone calls. Thank you both for pushing us when we felt like throwing in the towel and for recognizing that what we had to say was relevant and important.

About the Authors

Heather Stewart is a now retired Child Protection Worker who continues to teach in the Child and Youth Care program at local Colleges. She is a B.Sc. graduate of the Child Psychology program at the University of Toronto and a current Certified Professional Member of the OACYC. She is also Level II Personality Dimensions Facilitator and a Certified Life Skills Coach.

Heather has always had a passion for the "helping professions" and has been involved with children and youth for over 35 years. She has worked in various milieus and with various populations including, but not limited to, vocational rehabilitation, life skills coaching, FASD Ontario, Autism Ontario, Geneva Foundation, Ontario Shores Centre for Mental Health Science, child welfare, adoption, specialized adoption, kinship and post secondary education.

Richard Nash is a Child and Youth Care Practitioner currently employed at the Durham Children's Aid Society. For the past 8 years he has been teaching at Centennial College in the Child and Youth Practitioner Care program as a part time instructor and first year field placement supervisor. Richard has previously taught at Durham College in their Child and Youth Care Practitioner program.

At a very young age Richard realized that he wanted to work with children, youth and their families in a supportive and nurturing capacity. He has over 20 years of experience working in numerous milieus including child and adolescent mental health, residential, education and child protection.

Chapter 1: What is Child and Youth Care?

Real Life Story

Are you a babysitter? Are you an early childhood educator? Are you a Social Worker? Are you a PSW? These are some of the questions that we have been asked throughout our careers as CYC's. On the surface, it may appear that CYC's are glorified caregivers. However, when you look beyond the surface, there is so much more involved as a Child and Youth Care Practitioner.

You will be physically and verbally assaulted, spat upon, sworn at, kicked and degraded. However, you will also triumph over adversity, build relationships and impact a youth's life in ways you never thought possible. From this you will develop pride in your work, faith in your resiliency and confidence in your ability to affect change. This is why you chose to be a CYC!

Definition of a Child and Youth Care Practitioner

According to the Ontario Association of Child and Youth Care:

> "Child and youth care practitioners (Child and Youth Workers, Child Care Workers, Child and Youth Counsellors) provide front line supports to the most vulnerable children and youth, parents, partners within residential treatment facilities, schools, and their communities.
>
> **Child and youth care practitioners offer support in the life space and across sectors through:**
>
> - therapeutic relationships,
> - evidence based practice,
> - life space interventions,
> - social and life skill development,
> - problem solving methods,
> - restorative practices, and
> - after crisis management."

(**Source**: http://www.oacyc.org/legislation/)

Child and Youth Practitioners work to assist with the positive development and interactions of children, youth and their families in a variety of settings, including, but not limited to day care, educational institutions, developmental, parent and family education programs, in school programs, community mental health, residential programs, various treatment and early intervention programs, mental heath and rehabilitation programs, health care and justice programs.

Much of CYC practice involves client assessment and developing appropriate programming, and facilitating these programs in a planned environment or in the life space of the family. It also includes integrating developmental, preventative, and therapeutic requirements into the family's interactions and environment to contribute to the development of knowledge and practice. As a practitioner you will be responsible for participating in system interventions through hands on care, supervision, administration, education, research, consultation and advocacy (http://www.pitt.edu/~mattgly/CYCethics.html).

As a Child and Youth Practitioner, you will work in a variety of environments, with a variety of clients, all of whom will require your expertise and specialized skills.

According to Service Canada the employment market for the social service field, including Child and Youth Practitioners, is on the rise.

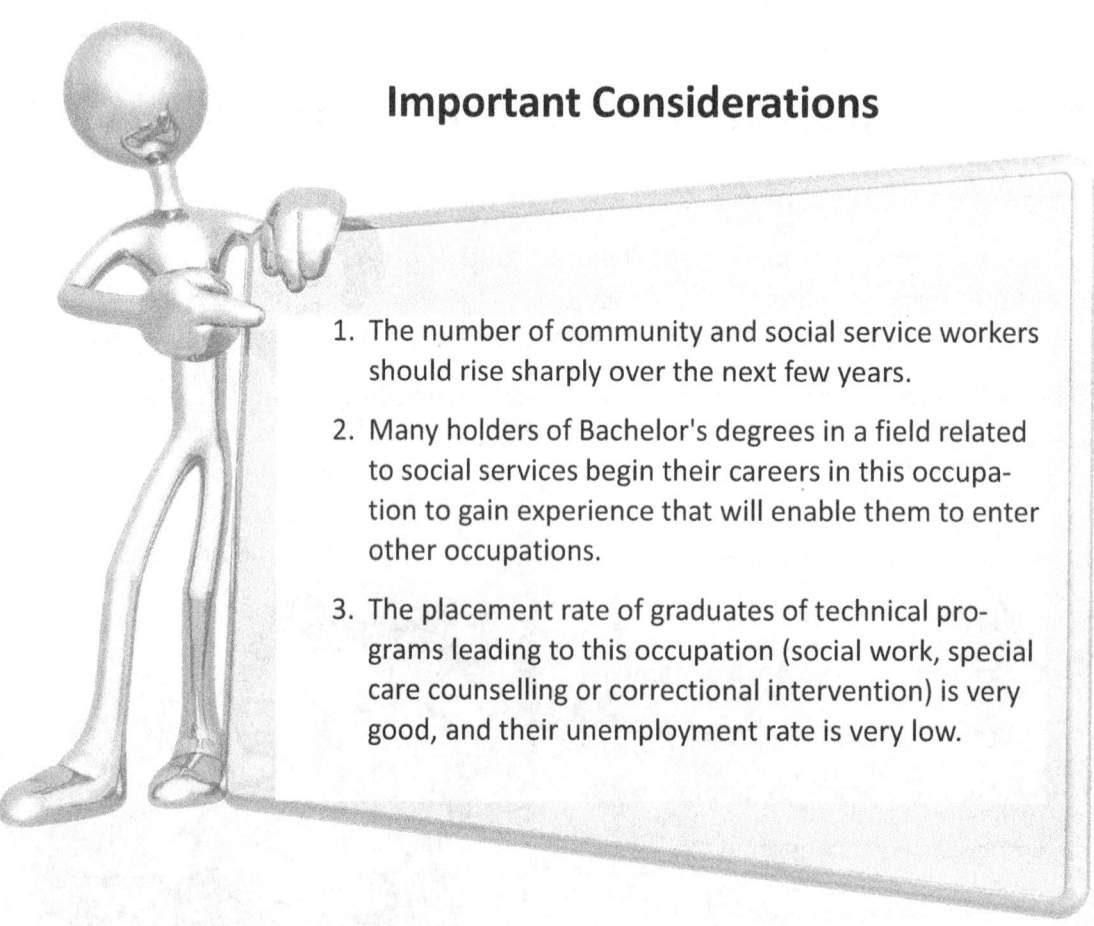

Important Considerations

1. The number of community and social service workers should rise sharply over the next few years.

2. Many holders of Bachelor's degrees in a field related to social services begin their careers in this occupation to gain experience that will enable them to enter other occupations.

3. The placement rate of graduates of technical programs leading to this occupation (social work, special care counselling or correctional intervention) is very good, and their unemployment rate is very low.

Statistics 4212 - Community and Social Service Workers

Main Labour Market Indicators

In the following table, indicators such as the growth rate, yearly variation in employment, yearly attrition and total annual requirements are forecasts generated by economists from Service Canada, Quebec region. The data source for employment is Statistics Canada's Labour Force Survey. The volumes of unemployment insurance beneficiaries come from Employment and Social Development Canada (ESDC)'s administrative data. All of the data are rounded.

	Unit Group 4212	All Occupations
Employment, average 2011-2013	30,350	3,990,050
Employment Insurance claimants in 2013	350	80,700
Average Annual Growth Rate 2014-2018	2.0%	0.7%
Annual Employment Variation 2014-2018	650	26,500

Employment Distribution

The data from the following employment distribution tables come from Statistics Canada's 2011 National Household Survey (NHS).

	Unit Group 4212	All Occupations
Employment by Gender		
Male	27.7%	51.9%
Female	75.3%	48.1%
Employment by Age		
15 - 24 years	14.2%	13.3%
25 - 44 years	52.2%	42.7%
45 - 64 years	32.5%	41.1%
65 years and over	1.0%	2.8%

	Unit Group 4212	**All Occupations**
Employment Status		
Full-time	78.3%	81.2%
Part-time	21.7%	18.8%
Annual Average Income	$39,300	$50,300
$0 - $19,999	10.2%	13.3%
$20,000 - $49,999	68.2%	48.0%
$50,000 and over	21.6%	38.8%
Employment by Highest Level of Schooling		
Less than high-school	4.5%	12.1%
High-school	11.3%	20.3%
Post-secondary	49.8%	44.2%
Bachelors	34.5%	23.4%

Source: http://www.servicecanada.gc.ca

Today's youth are growing up in a complex, anxiety inducing environment. The incidence of mental health issues is on the rise in children and adolescence along with many other factors that compromise the positive growth and development of children, youth and families. Your chosen career of Child and Youth Care Practitioner will be a valued asset for years to come.

Throughout your education and ongoing into your career, you will be trained to develop therapeutic relationships with high risk youth and their families.

As a Child and Youth Care Practitioner you will be guided by a code of ethics and standards of practice (further explored in Chapter 3) that, at a minimum, ensure accountability and educational compliance.

You will undoubtedly find this career challenging, frustrating and upsetting, however, you will also find it rewarding, satisfying and fulfilling. During the challenging times, recall that one case, that one child, that one success to fuel your fire and passion. Your efforts will remind you why you became a Child and Youth Care Practitioner.

History of Child and Youth Care: Excerpts from A New Profession by Karen Gilmour-Barrett and Susan Pratt

The history of professional child and youth work dates back to 1801 in France with Jean Marc Gaspard Itard and Mme. Guérin.

In Ontario, child and youth counsellors (CYCs) have been working with disadvantaged and troubled youth since the mid-1800s. A century later, in the late 1950s, formal training programs were established and CYCs became known officially as Child Care Workers. More recently the title has changed to Child and Youth Care Practitioners, which seems to better reflect the scope of work involved in the profession.

In 1957, Thistletown Hospital was set up as a treatment and teaching hospital dealing with emotionally disturbed children. Staffing the hospital was problematic because very few people in the Toronto area could actually claim experience in working with disturbed children in a residential setting. John Rich, psychiatrist, and Lon Lawson, social worker, were working at the Toronto Psychiatric Hospital (later to become the Clarke Institute of Psychiatry). Dr. Rich was approached to set up the Thistletown Hospital for disturbed children. He enlisted Lon Lawson. Together they agreed to give it a try.

Lon Lawson became the first Chief of Child Care Work at Thistletown Hospital. He has written with a good deal of wit and sage humor about some of the highlights of the first two years of the Thistletown experience. According to his account, Dr. Rich partially solved the staffing problem by writing to his friends in England and inviting them to come over.

Bringing staff from England was a comparatively easy matter. At that time all English people believed that the streets of Toronto were paved with gold, and in addition, the persecution of the dissenters by the Church of England was at its height. Within a few days the docks of Plymouth and Liverpool were crowded with engineers in their quaint Puritan costumes, and doctors, teachers, social workers and occupational therapists set sail for Canada. Most of them travelled by steerage, and had a very imperfect grip on the language and customs of the New World. The newcomers to Halifax were escorted to a colonist car, loaded on snowshoes, and supplied with rifles, sacks of flour, copies of the Observer and other necessities, and the long trip to Thistletown began.

Meanwhile, the problem of recruiting people to work directly with the children remained. These first two pioneers strongly felt that psychiatric nurses and attendants were not the answer. Lon was very clear about nursing being inappropriate training for working with disturbed children. He felt that nurses focused on ward control. They wanted a professional who regarded the ward not as a quiet place where children knew what they should do and what they shouldn't do; but a place where children could enjoy themselves, where they could find things to do that would interest them. Normal activities of living were what Lon thought should form the basis of treatment. This was integral to the conception of the future child care worker. Thistletown would be staffed with child care workers who would receive an initial training program. Lawson and Rich were able to sell this idea to the Ministry of Health. Their idea was contained in one of the earliest definitions of a Child Care Practitioner submitted by Thistletown Hospital and by the Ontario Civil Service Commission. These employees act as ward counsellors, guide children in a wide variety of day-to-day activities, such as dressing, washing, eating, play, sports, and hobbies. They live in an intimate daily relationship in order to provide a milieu of intensive, involved care. They must be able to recognize the underlying significance of various forms of behavior so that they can document and deal with behaviour in a general framework decided on by the psychiatrist for that particular child. They must be able to recognize the meaning of abnormal behavior and to provide an environment which is therapeutic for that particular child for that particular moment. This required insight into emotional disturbances and also considerable skill in real life situations.

Therefore, anyone coming into work directly with the children, even if they had had previous training in another profession such as nursing, would have to take either a two- or, as in the latter case, a one-year training course. They would be paid for the time they spent in the course and the work they were doing when they were students. Lawson and Rich put ads in the Toronto newspapers and started to interview and recruit people. The people who came in those few months; firemen, pharmaceutical supply people, nurses, and mothers of grown children, and those who came in the next one or two years later, were very unusual and very brave individuals. They were starting out on a new career in an unknown field with only promises of a future and the formidable task of caring for disturbed children.

Several of these people later contributed pioneering work in other locations: starting courses in child care work; directing treatment; taking further training in the field; or making a unique contribution in another field, such as in working with crippled children or in specialized teaching.

Source: https://www.oacyc.org/history-of-child-and-youth-care-in-ontario

Scope of Practice

As a Child and Youth Care Practitioner you will likely work in a number of different environments with a variety of individuals who have varying needs.

Child and Youth Care Practice focuses on infants, children, and adolescents, including those with special needs, within the context of the family, the community, and the life span.

As a Child and Youth Care Practitioner you will be assessing client and program needs, designing and implementing programs and planned environments, integrating developmental programs, preventive, and therapeutic requirements into the life space, contributing to the development of knowledge and practice, and participating in systems interventions through direct care, supervision, administration, teaching, research, consultation, and advocacy.

You will also provide psycho-social interventions as the primary method of facilitating change with the majority of your work occurring in the life-space of the child, youth and family.

The life space setting of the child/youth will vary and can range from group home, foster home, treatment facility or interventions within their own home.

The practice of Child and Youth Care begins with the development of a therapeutic relationship within any environment. The purpose of the services provided by Child and Youth Care Practitioners, are to encourage and foster the development of healthy children, youth and families.

The work you will be doing is unique to Child and Youth Care Practitioners. Regardless of the actual setting, your practice will be reflected in the ways that you use relational practice and create a therapeutic milieu.

The interventions you will provide will consider the life space of the child/youth and family, and will take place within that life space. While the work that Child and Youth Care Practitioners do is similar to Social Workers, the ways that Child and Youth Care Practitioners intervene, is specific to Child and Youth Care practice and education. According to James Anglin (2001), there are five key elements of the Child and Youth Care profession:

Interventions

1. Child and Youth Care is primarily focussed on the growth and development of children and youth.

Although you may find yourself engaging with families and community organizations, your focus will be on the development of the child and youth with whom you are working.

2. Child and Youth Care is concerned with the totality of a child's functioning.

Child and Youth Care Practitioner utilize an holistic approach to their work. The focus is on the child/youth during a certain portion of their life cycle with the goal being to improve their ability to transfer their learning and strategies to other facets of their life. Child and Youth Care Practitioners are an integral part of a child/youth's therapeutic team and will consistently work with a variety of other professionals.

3. Child and Youth Care has developed a model of social competence rather than a pathology-based orientation to child development.

"This is sometimes referred to as a "developmental perspective." Child and Youth Care Workers believe that children are doing the best they can at any given moment, and that we can best assist the child by working towards the "next step," by building on existing strengths and abilities. The writings of such pioneers as Pestalozzi, Montessori, Korczak and Makarenko demonstrate this orientation" (Anglin, 2001).

4. Child and Youth Care is based on (but not restricted to) direct, day to day work with children and youth in their environment.

Unique to Child and Youth Care Practitioner, is that their work is not confined to a single setting, meeting or intervention. The job requires dedication and tenacity to enable you to work at varying hours, in a variety of settings. Some CYC Practitioners move on to administrative, or supportive roles such as supervising, policy-making and training, however the root and heart of the CYC practitioner comes from the direct care, front line work.

5. Child and Youth Care involves the development of therapeutic relationships with children, their families, and other informal and formal helpers.

The centre of Child and Youth Care work is the therapeutic relationship. This relationship combines "the richness of intimacy of the personal with the rigour and goal-directedness of the professional. Developing a positive therapeutic relationship requires a combination of knowledge, skills and elements of self. This work requires a high level of ongoing personal and professional development (Anglin, 2001).

Scope of Practice

The Child and Youth Care scope of practice recognizes that the Child and Youth Care professional creates, supports and maintains care plans that consider theories of development and implements these care plans in consideration of the contexts within which the child, youth or family exists. While other professionals, who work alongside Child and Youth Care Practitioners also consider theories of development and contexts in their care of children, youth and families, the Child and Youth Care professionals are distinct in their collaborative and team efforts. Since many of the children and youth that Child and Youth Care Practitioners work with will be placed within residential group care, the team dynamic and collaborative component of the work is vital.

Child and Youth professionals provide services for children and youth who are often under-serviced by other professions, for example, adolescents involved in the sex trade, teenaged parents, young substance abusers, sexually, physically and emotionally abused or neglected children and youth and their families, and adolescent sex offenders to name a few such populations.

The range and scope of therapeutic methods for intervention may be similar to a variety of other professionals since the existing theories (behavioural, cognitive, developmental, solution focused) are similar in most helping professions. The use of these theories by a Child and Youth Care Practitioners is distinct however. The application of the theory must be adapted to a life space.

When a child or youth is working with a psychologist, for example, the theory being considered or applied will take place within an office and the child or youth will be asked to generalize to their life space. The Child and Youth Counsellor who may be in collaboration with the psychologist is able to adapt the theory to the life space and help the child, youth or family with generalization. At times, there are few or no collaborating partners and the Child and Youth Counsellor will create care plans within the life space environment considering the context and the use of his or her relationship with the child, youth or family (http://www.cycaa.com/wp-content/uploads/2015/06/SCOPE-OF-PRACTICE.pdf).

As a Child and Youth Care Practitioner, your scope of practice will include, but will not be limited to:

1. Creating and maintaining relationships with children, youth and their family's while applying principles of practice and respecting their individual life space, cultural and human diversity.

2. Assessing and developing plans that address the unique needs and strengths of the individual child or youth while ensuring that their developmental, environmental, physical, emotional social and mental health challenges are constantly at the forefront.

3. Utilizing the information gathered from family relationships, social services, and other community systems and assessing it's impact on the children, youth and families, to create an holistic care plan that will reduce systemic barriers.

4. Planning, implementing and evaluating interventions using evidence-based practices in the areas of therapeutic milieu and programming, and group work to promote resilience and to enhance development in children, youth and their families.

5. Supporting and advocating for the rights of the child, youth and their families while supporting an anti oppressive and culturally competent perspective.

6. Enhance the quality of service within your practice through communication, teamwork and organizational skills within the therapeutic team and community partners.

7. Ensuring that self care is a priority by engaging in self-enquiry, self awareness, and reflective practice to enhance your practice.

8. Support professionalism by using evidence based research, committing to ongoing professional development and professionalism.

Regardless of where your practice leads you or where you choose to focus your efforts, as a CYC, you will never be alone. You will have, at your fingertips, a plethora of support, knowledge and information.

There are a number of professional associations for Child and Youth Care Workers around the world. Below is a list of the Canadian Associations.

- Ontario Association of Child and Youth Counsellors
- Child and Youth Care Association Newfoundland Labrador
- Nova Scotia Child and Youth Care Workers Association
- Child and Youth Care Workers Association of Prince Edward Island
- Child and Youth Care Association of New Brunswick
- Quebec Association of Educators
- Child and Youth Care Workers Association of Manitoba
- Child and Youth Care Association of Alberta
- Child and Youth Care Association of British Columbia

To summarize, according to the Council of Canadian Child and Youth Care Association:

> The practice of Child and Youth Care occurs within the context of therapeutic relationships with children and youth who are experiencing difficulties in their lives. Intervention takes place within the family, the community and other social institutions, and centres on emotional, social and behavioural change and as well as daily life events.

> Child and Youth Care Practitioners work with children, youth and families with complex needs. They can be found in a variety of setting such as group homes and residential treatment centres, hospitals and community mental health clinics, community programs, parent

education and family support programs, as well as in private practice and juvenile justice programs. Child and Youth Care Practitioners specialize in the development and implementation of therapeutic programs and planned environments, and the utilization of daily life events to facilitate change. At the core of all effective child and youth care practice is the focus on therapeutic relationships, the application of theory and research about human growth and development to promote the optimal physical, psycho-social, spiritual, cognitive and emotional development of young people towards a healthy and pro adulthood; and a focus on strengths and assets rather than pathology.

Source: (http://www.garthgoodwin.info/Scope_of_Practice.pdf).

You have chosen a field that will be both rewarding and challenging, however, if you remember these 3 words: connecting, transforming, and caring, and their meaning, you will continue to have a successful fulfilling career.

By Connecting - really seeing the good in someone - we can help them begin to trust. And by learning to trust and to see themselves through someone else, a person can be transformed. When they learn to care and to connect, they can care for others.

Personal Qualities

Why did you choose this field? What qualities do you possess that make you feel you would be a good Child and Youth Practitioner? Helping children, youth and their families might be something that comes naturally to you. Friends and family members may have encouraged you to enroll in the CYC program because of your giving personality. Whatever the reasons for your enrollment into a CYC program, it is important for you to know what brought you here. As a CYC student you will have the opportunity to engage with children, youth and their families in many different environments and under many different circumstances. Some of what you will encounter may bring forth very personal responses/reactions of your own, especially if your experiences are unresolved. For example, how will you respond to a child that discloses that he/she has been abused by a parent if this is something that you too have experienced? Will your experience prevent you from being supportive or will it make you become overly protective of your client?

1. Self-Awareness

You will need to know your triggers and become aware of what themes might evoke an emotional response from you. If you are comfortable to do so, it would be in your best interest to have a discussion with your professor near the beginning of the course/program so they are aware of your history. You will not have to go into specific details but the more your professor knows, the more she/he/they can help and support you towards your academic success. You can also utilize your school's Health and Wellness program if you feel that you could benefit from more support.

Many people choose to work in the CYC field because they have experienced some form of trauma either as a child, youth or adolescent. Others may have experienced partner violence at a later age and now want to ensure that the victims they will be working with, are able to ensure the safety of their children. If the reasons that you chose this field are stemming from your own past experiences, it is extremely important for you to know what may trigger you. It is equally important for you not to take this program as a means to address your own trauma. We've taught classes in which students became so emotional during group discussions regarding sexual and/or physical abuse that they literally got up from their seats and left the classroom in tears. At the beginning of a course we would routinely review the course outline. In doing so we recall discussing a particular movie that we were scheduled to watch which pertained to severe sexual and physical abuse and neglect. The students were required to answer a series of questions that pertained to the movie. This assignment was worth a significant portion of their final grade. Several students approached us after class to inform us that they preferred not to watch the movie due to their own unresolved trauma. How can you guide and support a client through their trauma if you haven't worked through your own? Can you be therapeutically supportive to a client that has experienced abuse if you have not challenged yourself to address your own trauma?

2. Empathy

Empathy is the understanding and sharing of the emotions and experiences of another person. (Merriam-Webster, 2013, p. 143). Empathy should not be confused with sympathy.

To sympathize with someone means that you are feeling sorry for that person or what they are experiencing. We cannot necessarily help our clients/families by simply sympathizing with them because there is really no action in sympathy. When you show empathy, try to imagine how you would feel if you were to experience what the client is experiencing. Imagine what emotions you might experience/feel. The ultimate goal of showing empathy is to be able to share your client's experience and then assist them with formulating steps/plan to address the issues or concerns.

3. Judgment

In the CYC field we are often provided with background information regarding the clients/families that we work with prior to meeting them in person. A lot of the times this clientele may have a history with Child Protection Services, Mental Health Services and/or Behavioural Services. Information is usually shared amongst these services and quite often biases and preconceived notions are made even before we have met these clients. The best advice we can give you is to leave your judgements at the door and give your client's/families the chance to start with a clean slate. There might be circumstances in which your clients/families may not have had positive relationships with certain workers and vice/versa. Sometimes there are personality conflicts. Sometimes the client may prefer to work with a male rather than a female. These situations can result in poor working conditions between you and the client/family. When this occurs, workers may tend to communicate to other workers that the client/s are difficult to work with. For the new worker, it is very easy to base your opinion/judgment of the client on what you've been told by the previous worker rather than meeting the client and formulating your own opinion. By no means are we saying that you should totally ignore anything that you've been told by past or current workers especially if there are safety concerns however; we want you to keep an open mind and remember that you must allow your client/family to present themselves to you as if you are hearing their story for the first time.

4. Listening

Listening is an underrated skill that is pivotal to a Child and Youth Care Practitioner. It is the listening during those moments you may consider to be "non-therapeutic" where you can gain the most insight into your client. Listening is vital to forming relationships and is critical to overall relationship success. As an active listener, you will be paying attention to facial expressions, body language and non-verbal cues (Adler, Rolls, and Proctor II, 2015, p. 178).

Mindless Listening Vs. Mindful Listening

It is important to delineate between hearing and listening. Hearing is the physical process that occurs when sound waves are transmitted to the brain. Listening is when the brain gives these sounds meaning. People often hear without listening which is reflected by the term mindless listening; they screen out any information they deem to be annoying or uninteresting. Mindful listening involves providing the speaker with your full attention and processing what they are saying (or not saying) on an ongoing basis (Adler, Rolls, and Proctor II, 2015, p. 178).

Five Elements in the Listening Process

1. **Hearing**: The physiological dimension of listening when sound waves strike the ear at certain frequencies and loudness

2. **Attending**: The process of filtering out some messages and focusing on others.

3. **Understanding**: Occurs when sense is made of a message.

4. **Responding**: Giving observable feedback to a speaker. Good listeners keep eye contact, react with appropriate facial expressions and give verbal feedback.

5. **Remembering**: The ability to recall information. People only remember 50% of what they just heard even when making an effort to listen. After 8 hours, 50% drops to 35%. What we do remember is referred to as the residual message (Adler, Rolls, and Proctor II, 2015, p. 189-190).

Five Tips for being a Better Listener

1. **Talk less**: Give feedback, but resist temptation to dominate and shift conversation to your ideas.

2. **Remove Distraction**
   - external: ie) ringing phone
   - internal: ie) empty stomach

3. **Don't Judge Prematurely**: Make sure you understand before you evaluate

4. **Look for Key Ideas:** When a lot of information is being shared to look for central ideas to streamline content

5. **Exercise Patience**: Of all the personal qualities that are beneficial to have as a competent,

successful CYC practitioner, patience is probably the most important one. On a daily basis you will find yourself confronted by challenging and frustrating situations and individuals. As a CYC you must be able to maintain an air of calm when dealing with children youth and families whose emotions and behaviors are at a heightened state.

> "Learn the art of patience. Apply discipline to your thoughts when they become anxious over the outcome of a goal. Impatience breeds anxiety, fear, discouragement and failure. Patience creates confidence, decisiveness, and a rational outlook, which eventually leads to success."
>
> ~ Bryan Adams

Employability Skills

There are several skills that you will need to develop throughout your education and experience as a Child and Youth Care Practitioner.

Essential Employability Skills will help you perform the tasks for a Child and Youth Care Practitioner, provide you with a foundation for learning other skills, and enhance your ability to innovate and adapt to work place changes.

The essential skills required by a CYC will likely be specified in your course outline; however there are several skills that you will need to ensure you have to become successfully employed.

There are **11 Essential Employability Skills** outcomes identified by the Ministry Program Standard. Employers want to know that you have the ability to:

1. Communicate clearly, concisely and correctly in the written, spoken, and visual form that fulfills the purpose and meets the needs of your clientele/practice

    - The job of a CYC is based upon communication. You must be able to make yourself heard in a clear, concise manner to ensure that the children youth and families, for which you are working, clearly understand your goals, direction and desired outcome. This can be achieved by utilizing proper grammar, language, spelling and medium, to share your message. As a CYC you will potentially be required to write daily reports, plans of care, incident reports, and court papers, to name a few. Any and all of the documents you will write could possibly be utilized in a court of law, therefore it is extremely important that your communication be clear, appropriate, detailed and accurate.

2. Respond to written, spoken, or visual messages in a manner that ensures effective communication

    - It is very important to remember that you will be an important part of an interdisciplinary team, a work team and a support system the children, youth and families you are working with will rely on you to relay important information I a timely, factual manner utilizing the most appropriate medium all the while ensuring client confidentiality.

3. Execute mathematical operations accurately

- Although math may not seem like an essential skill for a CYC you will definitely need basic math skills to perform your job. You may be required to create schedules ensuring all shift hours are covered, you may be required to calculate wages, or allowances for youth, you may be required to assist a youth with their math homework, or you may need to understand measurements when facilitating a baking group with your clients. All of these activities, and many more that you will perform during the life of your practice, will require fine-tuned basic mathematical skills.

4. Apply a systematic approach to solve problems

- Child and Youth care is, at its core, about solving problems. You, as a CYC, need to have a complete understanding of problem solving methods and secure confidence in the execution of these steps. There are several problem solving models that you will likely have learned throughout your education and your "style" may be mixture of a few of these models, however you must ensure, regardless of what process you find works most effectively for you, that you are able to think through the problem and execute the process with confidence and certainty. Not to say that every problem you are presented with, you will be able to solve, but you will have used a method that you will be able to reflect upon the result and backtrack o see where you might have had the opportunity, or have the future opportunity, to do things somewhat differently.

5. Use a variety of thinking skills to anticipate and solve problems

- You will find as you work with certain children, youth and families, over a period of time, that you are able to begin to anticipate their issues, responses and outcomes. However, especially when working with a new family, you will need to think about their use of language, their responses, their requests and their triggers to allow you to provide them with a positive, professional and hopefully successful experience.

6. Locate, select, organize and document information using appropriate technology and information systems

- One of the first things you should do as a new employee is familiarize yourself with the policies, procedures, scheduling and workings of your new environment. You should be able to locate information as you need it using the appropriate venues and resources. Each employer/agency will potentially have its own computerized data and recording system. You will need to become proficient in their technology and information systems.

7. Analyze, evaluate, and apply relevant information from a variety of sources

- As a child and youth care practitioner you will constantly be assessing, analyzing and evaluating your practice, your clients, your families and your work. You should utilize any and all resources to assist you in this process including, but not limited to the CYC organization within your area, your co-workers, your mentors, educators and academic sources. You will find that you will take tools from a variety of sources, and develop your own style that works within your employer's parameters, standards of practice and code of ethics.

8. Show respect for the diverse opinions, values, belief systems, and contribution of others

   - Developing respect, cultural competence and anti-oppressive values will ensure that you are meeting all of your clients/families' needs to the best of your ability, while taking their cultural practices and beliefs into consideration. You will also be responsible for ensuring that you create a safe climate for not only your clients, but your co-workers as well. Everyone should feel safe expressing or sharing their views and opinions without fear of judgement or retribution.

9. Interact with others in groups or teams in ways that contribute to effective working relationships and the achievement of goals

   - As a CYC you will spend much of your day in groups or working within a team. Whether you are attending a staff meeting, facilitating a group with children, youth and families or being a supportive member of a team, the end result should be the achievement of a common goal. During the process, effective work ethic, respect and self-awareness will be keys to a successful outcome. Remember, a successful outcome does not always mean that the final decision/goal was in your favour, it means that the final decision is in the best interest of the majority.

10. Manage the use of time and other resources to complete projects

    - Throughout your day as a CYC you will undoubtedly be pulled in several different directions with several different deadlines and several different responsibilities, and they will all present as having the same level of importance. How will you manage these multiple responsibilities? Time management and prioritization is key to being a successful CYC. Not only do you have the responsibility of meeting your client's needs, you must also meet the expectations of your employer while ensuring that you are maintaining a certain level of self-care. As you progress in your practice you will find what works and does not work for you. It is best to find a system, and stick to it, while factoring in some level of flexibility for the unforeseen circumstances that undoubtedly will occur throughout your day.

11. Take responsibility for one's own actions, decisions and consequences

    - In short, be accountable. Take responsibility for your actions, take time to reflect and utilize that reflection to improve your practice.

You will find that as you expand your experience, and develop your skills as a Child and Youth Care Practitioner, your goal will be to become a valued employee within your agency and amongst your co-workers.

Chapter 1 – Let's Reflect

Why did you choose Child and Youth Care as your profession? Include your thoughts and processes that brought you to this profession. When did you decide to pursue a CYC career? Was there a pivotal moment that solidified your choice?

Chapter 1 - Worksheet

1. What is your definition of a CYC?
2. What would your client base, as a CYC look like?
3. Where did the profession of Child and Youth Care begin?
4. Who is credited with the development of the CYC profession in Toronto, Ontario?
5. What do CYC practitioners promote in reference to their scope of practice?
6. What are the 3 words that are referenced at the end of chapter 1 and what do they mean to you?
7. What may be a trigger for you throughout this program?
8. List 4 personal qualities that a CYC should possess.
9. How many essential employability skill outcomes are there according to Ministry Program Standards?
10. List 5 employability skills a CYC should possess.

Chapter 1 – Checklist

What is your preferred client population and in what setting? (Review this list frequently as your preferences may change)

- ☐ infants (0-2 years)
- ☐ Toddlers (2-4)
- ☐ Latency age (4-12 years)
- ☐ Teen (13-18 years)
- ☐ School
- ☐ Hospital
- ☐ Residential/group home
- ☐ Child protection
- ☐ One on one

I possess the following personal qualities recommended for a CYC:

- ☐ Self-awareness
- ☐ Empathy
- ☐ Non-judgemental
- ☐ Listening

- ☐ Mindful listening
- ☐ Patience

I currently have the following essential employability skills: (review frequently as you develop new skills)

- ☐ Communicate clearly, concisely and correctly in the written, spoken, and visual form that fulfills the purpose and meets the needs of your clientele/practice
- ☐ Respond to written, spoken, or visual messages in a manner that ensures effective communication
- ☐ Execute mathematical operations accurately
- ☐ Apply a systematic approach to solve problems
- ☐ Use a variety of thinking skills to anticipate and solve problems
- ☐ Locate, select, organize and document information using appropriate technology and information systems
- ☐ Analyze, evaluate, and apply relevant information from a variety of sources
- ☐ Show respect for the diverse opinions, values, belief systems, and contribution of others
- ☐ Interact with others in groups or teams in ways that contribute to effective working relationships and the achievement of goals
- ☐ Manage the use of time and other resources to complete projects
- ☐ Take responsibility for one's own actions, decisions and consequences

References and Resources

Anglin, James. (2001). Child and youth care: A unique profesion. *CYC-Oline*, December 2001 (35).

Ontario Association of Child and Youth Care. (n.d.). *Legislation*. https://www.oacyc.org/legislation

Mattingley, Maartha A. (n.d.). *Ethics of child and youth care professionals*. http://www.pitt.edu/~mattgly/CYCethics.html

Statistics Canada. (2011) *National Household Survey* (NHS). http://www.servicecanada.gc

Chapter 2: What are Child and Youth Care Competencies?

Real Life Story

As CYC students we often questioned why we needed to learn this boring, theoretical information. We thought we'd never use and it was just filling space.

However, as practitioners we now recognize the value of the information and the necessity to learn it. We learned that the competencies are the attitudes that a good CYC should consistently demonstrate and the contexts of the various environments where they should be demonstrated.

As you develop your skills and practice you will realize that you are utilizing these attitudes and working within these contexts without being consciously aware of it. It will come naturally and flow effortlessly. Believe us!! It's true!!!

Domains of Practice for Child and Youth Work

Carol Stuart developed the 7 domains of practice for Child and Youth work, which are outlined in her book, Foundations of Child and Youth Care. These domains were:

  I. Self

  II. Professionalism

  III. Communication

  IV. Normal and abnormal child and adolescent development

  V. Systems context

  VI. Relationships

  VII. Interventions

In 2010 The Association for Child and Youth Care Practice and Child and Youth Care Certification Board completed a document entitled "Competence of Professional Child and Youth Work Practitioners". It is from this document that the 5 competencies are derived. These 5 competencies overlap and were developed from the original 7 domains of practice, however The Child and Youth Care Program Standards refers to this document as their benchmark and point of reference for CYC standards in Ontario.

In order to maintain the consistency and integrity of the Child and Youth Care Competencies we have chosen to directly quote the Competencies for Professional Child and Youth Work Practitioners as outlined in the Child and Youth Care Certification Board document ©2010. It is important that you have an understanding of these competencies and ensure that you are able to achieve and implement them throughout your practice.

The Child and Youth Care Professional demonstrates the following attitudes which underline all professional work:

√ Accepts the moral and ethical responsibility inherent in practice

√ Promotes the well-being of children, youth and families in a context of respect and collaboration

√ Values care as essential for emotional growth, social competence, rehabilitation, and treatment

√ Celebrates the strengths generated from cultural and human diversity

√ Values individual uniqueness

√ Values family, community, culture and human diversity as integral to the developmental and interventive process

√ Believes in the potential and empowerment of children, youth, family and community

√ Advocates for the rights of children, youth, and families

√ Promotes the contribution of professional Child and Youth Care to society

The competencies are organized across five domains:

I. Professionalism

II. Cultural & human diversity

III. Applied human development

IV. Relationship & communication

V. Developmental practice methods

I. Professionalism

Professional practitioners are generative and flexible; they are self-directed and have a high degree of personal initiative. Their performance is consistently reliable.

They function effectively both independently and as a team member. Professional practitioners are knowledgeable about what constitutes a profession, and engage in professional and personal development and self-care.

The professional practitioner is aware of the function of professional ethics and uses professional ethics to guide and enhance practice and advocates effectively for children, youth, families, and the profession.

A. Foundational Knowledge

- History, structure, organization of Child and Youth Care
- Resources and activities of Child and Youth Care
- Current and emergent trends in society, services, and in Child and Youth Care
- Structure and function of codes of ethics applicable to practice which includes the Standards for Practice of North American Child and Youth Care Professionals
- Accepted boundaries in professional practice
- Stress management and wellness practices
- Strategies to build a professional support network
- Significance of advocacy and an array of advocacy strategies
- Relevant laws, regulations, legal rights and licensing procedures governing practice

B. Professional Competencies

1. Awareness of the profession

    a. access the professional literature

    b. access information about local and national professional activities

    c. stay informed about current professional issues, future trends and challenges in one's area of special interest

    d. contribute to the ongoing development of the field

2. Professional development and behavior

    a. Value orientation

        (1) state personal and professional values and their implications for practice including how personal and professional beliefs, values and attitudes influence interactions

        (2) state a philosophy of practice that provides guiding principles for the design, delivery, and management of services

    b. Reflection on one's practice and performance

        (1) evaluate own performance to identify needs for professional growth

        (2) give and receive constructive feedback

    c. Performance of organizational duties

        (1) demonstrate productive work habits

            (a) know and conform to workplace expectations relating to attendance, punctuality, sick and vacation time, and workload management

(b) personal appearance and behavior reflect an awareness of self as a professional as well as a representative of the organization

d. Professional boundaries

(1) recognize and assess own needs and feelings and keeps them in perspective when professionally engaged

(2) model appropriate interpersonal boundaries

e. Staying current

(1) keep up-to-date with developments in foundational and specialized areas of expertise

(2) identify and participate in education and training opportunities

3. Personal Development and Self Care

a. Self awareness

(1) recognize personal strengths and limitations, feelings and needs

(2) separate personal from professional issues

b. Self care

(1) incorporate 'wellness' practices into own lifestyle

(2) practices stress management

(3) build and use a support network

4. Professional Ethics

a. describe the functions of professional ethics

b. apply the process of ethical decision making in a proactive manner

c. integrate specific principles and standards from relevant code of ethics to specific professional problems

d. carries out work tasks in a way that conforms to professional ethical principles and standards

5. Awareness of Law and Regulations

a. access and apply relevant local, state/provincial and federal laws, licensing regulations and public policy

b. describe the legal responsibility for reporting child abuse and neglect and the consequences of failure to report

c. describe the meaning of informed consent and its application to a specific practice setting

d. use the proper procedures for reporting and correcting non-compliance

6. Advocacy

    a. demonstrate knowledge and skills in use of advocacy

    b. access information on the rights of children, youth and families including the United Nations Convention on the Rights of the Child

    c. describe the rights of children youth and families in relevant settings and systems advocate for the rights of children, youth, and families in relevant settings and systems

    d. describe and advocate for safeguards for protection from abuse including institutional abuse

    e. describe and advocate for safeguards for protection from abuse including organizational or workplace abuse

    f. advocate for protection of children from systemic abuse, mistreatment, and exploitation

---

As a new child and youth care practitioner, you may find that you will struggle with maintaining boundaries between yourself and your clients. Often you will be close in age to the youth you are working with and it can be difficult to maintain a level of professionalism at all times. It is at times like these that you must take a step back, remember your position and the responsibilities that come along with it and review the ethics and standards of practice to ensure that you are remaining professional at all times.

II. Cultural and Human Diversity

Professional practitioners actively promote respect for cultural and human diversity. The Professional Practitioner seeks self-understanding and has the ability to access and evaluate information related to cultural and human diversity. Current and relevant knowledge is integrated in developing respectful and effective relationships and communication and developmental practice methods. Knowledge and skills are employed in planning, implementing and evaluating respectful programs and services, and workplaces

A. Foundational Knowledge

The professional practitioner is well versed in current research and theory related to cultural and human diversity including the eight major factors which set groups apart from one another, and which give individuals and groups elements of identity: age, class, race, ethnicity, levels of ability, language, spiritual belief systems, educational achievement, and gender differences.

- Cultural structures, theories of change, and values within culture variations
- Cross cultural communication
- History of political, social, and economic factors which contribute to racism, stereotyping, bias and discrimination

- Variations among families and communities of diverse backgrounds
- Cultural and human diversity issues in the professional environment

B. Professional Competencies

1. Cultural and Human Diversity Awareness and Inquiry

    a. describe own biases

    b. describe interaction between own cultural values and the cultural values of others

    c. describe own limitations in understanding and responding to cultural and human differences and seeks assistance when needed

    d. recognize and prevent stereotyping while accessing and using cultural information

    e. access, and critically evaluate, resources that advance cultural understandings and appreciation of human diversity

    f. support children, youth, families and programs in developing cultural competence and appreciation of human diversity

    g. support children, youth, families and programs in overcoming culturally and diversity based barriers to services

2. Relationship and Communication Sensitive to Cultural and Human Diversity

    a. adjust for the effects of age, cultural and human diversity, background, experience, and development on verbal and non-verbal communication

    b. describe the non-verbal and verbal communication between self and others (including supervisors, clients, or peer professionals)

    c. describe the role of cultural and human diversity in the development of healthy and productive relationships

    d. employ displays of affection and physical contact that reflect sensitivity for individuality, age, development, cultural and human diversity as well as consideration of laws, regulations, policies, and risk

    e. include consideration of cultural and human diversity in providing for the participation of families in the planning, implementation and evaluation of services impacting them

    f. give information in a manner sensitive to cultural and human diversity

    g. contribute to the maintenance of a professional environment sensitive to cultural and human diversity

    h. establish and maintain effective relationships within a team environment by:

        (1) promoting and maintaining professional conduct;

        (2) negotiating and resolving conflict;

        (3) acknowledging and respecting cultural and human diversity; and

        (4) supporting team members

3. Developmental Practice Methods Sensitive to Cultural and Human Diversity

a. integrate cultural and human diversity understandings and sensitivities in a broad range of circumstances

b. design and implement programs and planned environments, which integrate developmental, preventive, and/or therapeutic objectives into the life space, through the use of methodologies and techniques sensitive to cultural and human diversity

    (1) provide materials sensitive to multicultural and human diversity

    (2) provide an environment that celebrates the array of human diversity in the world through the arts, diversity of personnel, program materials, etc.

    (3) recognize and celebrate particular calendar events which are culturally specific

    (4) encourage the sharing of such culture specific events among members of the various cultural groups

c. design and implement group work, counseling, and behavioral guidance with sensitivity to the client's individuality, age, development, and culture and human diversity

d. demonstrate an understanding of sensitive cultural and human diversity practice in setting appropriate boundaries and limits on behavior, including risk management decisions

---

As a child and youth care practitioner, you will be responsible for developing a level of cultural competence and participating in anti-oppressive practices. Your clientele will come from varied socio-economic, racial, cultural, and gender backgrounds (to name a few) and it is your responsibility to meet the children, youth and families you will be working with in their own life space. You can never know everything about each client that you will be working with, however you can do your best to have an understanding of the pieces that may impact their progress and your relationship based on their views, preferences and customs.

III. Applied human development

Professional practitioners promote the optimal development of children, youth, and their families in a variety of settings. The developmental-ecological perspective emphasizes the interaction between persons and their physical and social environments, including cultural and political settings.

Special attention is given to the everyday lives of children and youth, including those at risk and with special needs, within the family, neighborhood, school and larger social-cultural context. Professional practitioners integrate current knowledge of human development with the skills, expertise, objectivity and self-awareness essential for developing, implementing and evaluating effective programs and services.

A. Foundational Knowledge

The professional practitioner is well versed in current research and theory in human development with an emphasis on a developmental-ecological perspective.

- Lifespan human development
- Child and adolescent development as appropriate for the arena of practice, (including domains of cognitive, social-emotional, physiological, psycho-sexual, and spiritual development)
- Exceptionality in development (including at-risk and special needs circumstances such as trauma, child abuse/neglect, developmental psychopathology, and developmental disorders)
- Family development, systems and dynamics

B. Professional Competencies

1. Contextual-Developmental Assessment

   a. assess different domains of development across various contexts

   b. evaluate the developmental appropriateness of environments with regard to the individual needs of clients

   c. assess client and family needs in relation to community opportunities, resources, and supports

2. Sensitivity to Contextual Development in Relationships and Communication

   a. adjust for the effects of age, culture, background, experience, and developmental status on verbal and non-verbal communication

   b. communicate with the client in a manner which is developmentally sensitive and that reflects the clients' developmental strengths and needs

   (1) recognize the influence of the child/youth's relationship history on the development of current relationships

   (2) employ displays of affection and physical contact that reflect sensitivity for individuality, age, development, cultural and human diversity as well as consideration of laws, regulations, policies, and risks

   (3) respond to behavior while encouraging and promoting several alternatives for the healthy expression of needs and feelings

   c. give accurate developmental information in a manner that facilitates growth

   d. partner with family in goal setting and designing developmental supports and interventions

   e. assist clients (to a level consistent with their development, abilities and receptiveness) to access relevant information about legislation/regulations, policies/standards, as well as additional supports and services

3. Practice Methods that are Sensitive to Development and Context

   a. support development in a broad range of circumstances in different domains and contexts

   b. design and implement programs and planned environments including activities of daily living, which integrate developmental, preventive, and/or therapeutic objectives into the life space through the use of developmentally sensitive methodologies and techniques

   c. individualize plans to reflect differences in culture/human diversity, background, temperament, personality and differential rates of development across the domains of human development

   d. design and implement group work, counseling, and behavioral guidance, with sensitivity to the client's individuality, age, development, and culture

   e. employ developmentally sensitive expectations in setting appropriate boundaries and limits

   f. create and maintain a safe and growth promoting environment

   g. make risk management decisions that reflect sensitivity for individuality, age, development, culture and human diversity, while also insuring a safe and growth promoting environment

4. Access Resources That Support Healthy Development

   a. locate and critically evaluate resources which support healthy development

   b. empower clients, and programs in gaining resources which support healthy development

> As a Child and Youth Care Practitioner it is your responsibility to maintain a high level of understanding of human development. The children, youth and families you will be working with will be experiencing a variety of developmental stages and cognitive milestones. They may have diagnoses that preclude them from achieving certain levels of development, cognitive thought or behaviour. As a practitioner, you need to be aware and have an understanding of what age and stage your clients are at, not only based on their chronological age but their cognitive and physical developmental age, and you must tailor your therapeutic relationship to meet their needs.

IV. Relationship and Communication

Practitioners recognize the critical importance of relationships and communication in the practice of quality Child and Youth Care. Ideally, the service provider and client work in a collaborative manner to achieve growth and change.

'Quality first' practitioners develop genuine relationships based on empathy and positive regard. They are skilled at clear communication, both with clients and with other professionals. Observations and records are objective and respectful of their clients. Relationship and communication are considered in the context of the immediate environment and its conditions; the policy and legislative environment; and the historical and cultural environment of the child, youth or family with which the practitioner interacts.

A. Foundational Knowledge

- Characteristics of helping relationships
- Characteristics of healthy interpersonal relationships
- Cultural differences in communication styles
- Developmental differences in communication
- Communication theory (verbal & non-verbal)
- Group dynamics & teamwork theory
- Family dynamics & communication patterns (including attachment theory as it relates to communication style)

B. Professional Competencies

1. Interpersonal Communication

a. adjust for the effects of age, cultural and human diversity, background, experience, and development of verbal and non-verbal communication

b. demonstrate a variety of effective verbal and non-verbal communication skills including

  (1) use of silence

  (2) appropriate non-verbal communication

  (3) active listening

  (4) empathy and reflection of feelings

  (5) questioning skills

  (6) use of door openers to invite communication, and paraphrasing and summarization to promote clear communication

  (7) awareness and avoidance of communication roadblocks

c. recognize when a person may be experiencing problems in communication due to individual or cultural and human diversity history, and help clarify the meaning of that communication and to resolve misunderstandings

d. assist clients (to a level consistent with their development, abilities and receptiveness) to receive relevant information about legislation/regulations, policies/standards, and supports pertinent to the focus of service

e. provide for the participation of children/youth and families in the planning, implementation and evaluation of service impacting them

f. set appropriate boundaries and limits on the behavior using clear and respectful communication

g. verbally and non-verbally de-escalate crisis situations in a manner that protects dignity and integrity

2. Relationship Development

a. assess the quality of relationships in an ongoing process of self-reflection about the impact of the self in relationship in order to maintain a full presence and an involved, strong, and healthy relationship

b. form relationships through contact, communication, appreciation, shared interests, attentiveness, mutual respect, and empathy

c. demonstrate the personal characteristics that foster and support relationship development

d. ensure that, from the beginning of the relationship, applicable procedures regarding confidentiality, consent for release of information, and record keeping are explained and clearly understood by the parent/caregiver and by the child, as appropriate to developmental age. Follow those procedures in a caring and respectful manner

e. develop relationships with children, youth and families that are caring, purposeful, goal-directed and rehabilitative in nature; limiting these relationships to the delivery of specific services

f. set, maintain, and communicate appropriate personal and professional boundaries

g. assist clients to identify personal issues and make choices about the delivery of service

h. model appropriate interpersonal interactions while handling the activities and situation of the life-space

i. use structure, routines, and activities to promote effective relationships

j. encourage children, youth and families to contribute to programs, services, and support movements that affect their lives by sharing authority and responsibility

k. develop and communicate an informed understanding of social trends, social change and social institutions. Demonstrate an understanding of how social issues affect relationships between individuals, groups, and societies

l. identify community standards and expectations for behavior that enable children, youth and families to maintain existing relationships in the community

3. Family Communication

a. identify relevant systems/components and describe the relationships, rules and roles in the child/youth's social systems and develop connections among the people in various social systems

b. recognize the influence of the child's relationship history and help the child develop productive ways of relating to family and peers

c. encourage children and families to share folklore and traditions related to family and cultural background. Employ strategies to connect children to their life history and relationships

d. support parents to develop skills and attitudes which will help them to experience positive and healthy relationships with their children/youth

4. Teamwork and Professional Communication Skills

a. establish and maintain effective relationships within a team environment by: promoting and maintaining professional conduct; negotiating and resolving conflict; acknowledging individual differences; and, supporting team members

b. explain and maintain appropriate boundaries with professional colleagues

c. assume responsibility for collective duties and decisions including responding to team member feedback

d. use appropriate professional language in communication with other team members, consult with other team members to reach consensus on major decisions regarding services for children and youth and families

e. build cohesion among team members through active participation in team building initiatives

f. collect, analyze and present information in written and oral form by selecting and recording information according to identified needs, agency policies and guidelines. Accurately record relevant interactions and issues in the relationship

g. plan, organize, and evaluate interpersonal communications according to the identified need, context, goal of communication, laws/regulations, and ethics and involved. Choose an appropriate format, material, language, and style suitable to the audience

h. acknowledge and respect other disciplines in program planning, communication and report writing using multidisciplinary and interdisciplinary perspectives. Communicate the expertise of the profession to the team

i. establish and maintain a connection, alliance, or association with other service providers for the exchange or information and to enhance the quality of service

j. deliver effective oral and written presentations to a professional audience

k. demonstrate proficiency in using information technology for communication, information access, and decision-making

As a child and youth care practitioner you will find that communication is pivotal in everything you do; be it getting a message across to a youth, writing a letter to a community collateral or documenting case/shift notes. You must ensure that your message is clear, concise and understood by the receiver.

You will also need to obtain and develop a comprehensive understanding of the boundaries of a therapeutic relationship and ensue that you maintain a high level of professionalism when interacting with children, youth and families.

V. Developmental Practice Methods

Practitioners recognize the critical importance of developmental practice methods focused on the Child and Youth Care practice:

- Genuine Relationships,
- Health and Safety,
- Intervention Planning,
- Environmental Design and Maintenance,
- Program Planning and Activity Programming,
- Activities of Daily Living,
- Group Work, Counseling,
- Behavioral Guidance,
- Family (Caregiver) Engagement,
- Community Engagement.

These are designed to promote optimal development for children, youth, and families including those at-risk and with special needs within the context of the family, community and the lifespan.

A. Foundational Knowledge

- Health and safety
- Intervention theory and design
- Environmental design
- Program planning and activity programming including:
- Developmental rationales
- Basic strategies of program planning
- Specific developmental outcomes expected as a result of participating in activities
- Principles of activity programming (e.g., activity analysis, adaptation, strategies for involving youth in activities)
- Relationship of developmental processes to the activities of daily living (e.g., eating, grooming, hygiene, sleeping, rest)
- The significance of play activities
- Community resources for connecting children, youth and families with activity and recreational programs
- Behavioral guidance methods including conflict resolution, crisis management, life space interviewing
- Behavior management methods
- Counseling skills

- Understanding and working with groups
- Understanding and working with families
- Understanding and working with communities

B. Professional Competencies

1. Genuine Relationships

    a. recognize the critical importance of genuine relationships based on empathy and positive regard in promoting optimal development for children, youth, and families

    b. forming, maintaining and building upon such relationships as a central change strategy

2. Health and Safety

    a. environmental safety

        (1) participate effectively in emergency procedures in a specific practice setting and carry them out in a developmentally appropriate manner

        (2) incorporate environmental safety into the arrangement of space, the storage of equipment and supplies and the design and implementation of activities

    b. health

        (1) access the health and safety regulations applicable to a specific practice setting, including laws/ regulations related to disability

        (2) use current health, hygiene and nutrition practices to support health development and prevent illness

        (3) discuss health related information with children, youth and families as appropriate to a specific practice setting

    c. medications

        (1) access current information on medications taken by clients in a specific practice site

        (2) describe the medication effects relevant to practice

        (3) describe the rules and procedures for storage and administration of medication in a specific practice site, and participate as appropriate

    d. infectious diseases

        (1) access current information on infectious diseases of concern in a specific practice setting

        (2) describe the components relevant to practice

        (3) employ appropriate infection control practices

3. Intervention planning

    a. assess strengths and needs

    b. plan goals and activities which take agency mission and group objectives, individual histories and interests into account

   c. encourage child/youth and family participation in assessment and goal setting in intervention planning and the development of individual plans

   d. integrate client empowerment and support of strengths into conceptualizing and designing interventions

   e. develop and present a theoretical/empirical rational for a particular intervention or approach

   f. select and apply an appropriate planning model

   g. select appropriate goals or objectives from plans, and design activities, interactions, and management methods that support plans in an appropriate way

   h. work with client and team to assess and monitor progress and revise plan as needed

4. Environmental Design and Maintenance

   a. recognize the messages conveyed by environment

   b. design and maintain planned environments which integrate developmental, preventive, and interventive requirements into the living space, through the use of developmentally and culturally sensitive methodologies and techniques

   c. arrange space, equipment and activities in the environment to promote participation and prosocial behavior, and to meet program goals

   d. involve children, youth and families appropriately in space design, and maintenance

5. Program Planning and Activity Programming

   a. connect your own childhood activity experiences and skills, and adult interests and skills, to current work

   b. teach skills in several different domains of leisure activity

   c. assist clients in identifying and developing theirs strengths through activities and other experiences

   d. design and implement programs and activities which integrate age, developmental, preventive, and/or interventive requirements and sensitivity to culture and diversity

   e. design and implement challenging age, developmentally, and cultural and human diversity appropriate activity programs

      (1) perform an activity analysis

      (2) assess clients' interests, knowledge of and skill level in various activities

      (3) promotes clients participation in activity planning

      (4) select and obtain resources necessary to conduct a particular activity or activity program

      (5) perform ongoing (formative) and outcome (summative) evaluation of specific activities and activity programs

        f. adapt activities for particular individuals or groups

        g. locate and critically evaluate community resources for programs and activities and connect children, youth, and families to them

6. Activities of Daily Living

        a. integrate client's need for dignity, positive public image, nurturance, choice, self-management, and privacy into activities of daily living

        b. design, implement and support family members and caregivers to implement activities of daily living, which integrate age, developmental, preventive, and/or interventive requirements and sensitivity to culture and diversity

                (1) age and cultural and human diversity appropriate clothing

                (2) pleasant and inviting eating times that encourage positive social interaction

                (3) age and developmentally appropriate rest opportunities

                (4) clean and well maintained bathroom facilities that allow age and developmentally appropriate privacy and independence

                (5) personal space adequate for safe storage of personal belongings and for personal expression through decorations that do not exceed reasonable propriety

        c. design and maintain inviting, hygienic and well maintained physical environments and equipment and supplies which positively support daily activities

        d. encourage development of skills in activities of daily living

                (1) personal hygiene and grooming skills

                (2) developing and maintaining of areas related to daily living (e.g. maintaining living space, preparing and serving meals, cleanup)

                (3) socially appropriate behavior in activities of daily living: respecting other's privacy, expected grooming and dress for various occasions

7. Group Process

        a. assess the group development and dynamics of a specific group of children and youth

        b. use group process to promote program, group, and individual goals

        c. facilitate group sessions around specific topics/issues related to the needs of children/youth

        d. mediate in group process issues

8. Counseling

        a. recognize the importance of relationships as a foundation for counseling with children, youth and families

        b. has self-awareness and uses oneself appropriately in counseling activities

        c. able to assess a situation in the milieu or in individual interaction and select the appropriate medium and content for counseling

d. able to make appropriate inquiry to determine meaning of a particular situation to a child

e. assist other adults, staff, parents and caregivers in learning and implementing appropriate behavioral support and instruction

f. employ effective problem solving and conflict resolution skills

9. Behavior Guidance

a. assess client behavior including its meaning to the client

b. design behavioral guidance around level of client's understanding

c. assess the strengths and limitations of behavioral management methods

d. employ selected behavioral management methods, where deemed appropriate

e. assist other adults, staff, and parent and caregivers in learning and implementing appropriate behavioral guidance techniques and plans

f. give clear, coherent and consistent expectations; sets appropriate boundaries

g. evaluate and disengage from power struggles

h. employ genuine relationship to promote positive behavior

i. employ developmental and cultural/diversity understandings to promote positive behavior

j. employ planned environment and activities to promote positive behavior

k. employ at least one method of conflict resolution

l. employ principles of crisis management

    (1) describe personal response to crisis situations

    (2) describe personal strengths and limitations in responding to crisis situations

    (3) take self-protective steps to avoid unnecessary risks and confrontations

    (4) dress appropriately to the practice setting

    (5) employ a variety of interpersonal and verbal skills to defuse a crisis

    (6) describe the principles of physical interventions appropriate to the setting

    (7) conduct a life space interview or alternative reflective debriefing

10. Family and Caregiver Engagement

a. communicate effectively with family members

b. partner with family in goal setting and designing and implementing developmental supports and/or interventions

c. identify client and family needs for community resources and supports

d. support family members in accessing and utilizing community resources

e. advocate for and with family to secure and/or maintain proper services

11. Community Engagement

   a. access up to date information about service systems, support and advocacy resources, and community resources, laws, regulations, and public policy

   b. develop and sustain collaborative relationships with organizations and people

   c. facilitate client contact with relevant community agencies

There are five contexts within which quality practice occurs. These contexts may occur simultaneously or distinctly.

> It is important as a child and youth care practitioner that you are aware of the programming, activities and strategies that you will be implement to assist your client. You will need to employ the personal qualities recommended for a CYC such as empathy, listening and being non-judgemental, to ensure that you are meeting the client's needs and creating safe, viable and realistic plans.

1. The Self
2. Relationships
3. The Practice Milieu
4. The Organizational System
5. Culture

Each layer has a set of foundational attitudes that cross all of the domains of practice. The nature of each layer and the boundaries of its context are described below, followed by a depiction of the integrated framework in three-dimensional form. Following this is a brief description of the nature of integrated quality practice in each of the intersections of the domains of practice with the contexts of practice.

THE SELF

Within the context of the self, practice focuses on the use of self as a mediator of knowledge and skills. Practitioners have insight into the factors of their own development, the impact of self-factors on practice interventions, and the dialectic tension between using one's personhood in relationships and their inter-personal communication with a client. They are aware of and act on the limiting effect of professional client boundaries on the relationship. They are aware of their culture and its impact on their day to day practice and have a sense of identity as a professional. Foundational to Child and Youth Care is the use of self, but to make effective use of self in practice one must first be aware of and able to articulate the nature of the self.

RELATIONSHIPS

In the context of relationship, practice focuses on the form and nature of interpersonal relations, both with clients and with other practitioners. Practitioners actively develop relationships with others through communication and shared activities. They are conscious of the process of relationship development and actively consider how the psycho-social developmental status and culture of the other person and their own developmental history and culture influence the nature of any particular relationship. They are clear about the nature of personal and professional boundaries with clients and co-workers and respectful of the professional needs of others. All practice methods are implemented using the interpersonal relationship as a foundation from which development occurs.

MILIEU

The milieu is the central context within which Child and Youth Care practice occurs. The milieu is used to enhance the developmental trajectory of children, youth, and families that participate in it. In this context, practitioners are aware of the environment and the multiple interactions and activities occurring within that environment. They arrange environmental factors to offer quality care and plan their communication with an awareness of the activities of the milieu and the nature of interpersonal relationships within it. They are able to integrate individual members of the milieu into a group culture. They demonstrate professional behavior reflective of the nature of their practice setting. Practice milieus encompass many different settings as outlined by the current description of the field:

Professional practitioners promote the optimal development of children, youth, and their families in a variety of settings, such as early care and education, community-based child and youth development programs, parent education and family support, school-based programs, community mental health, group homes, residential centers, day and residential treatment, early intervention, home-based care and treatment, psychiatric centers, rehabilitation programs, pediatric health care, and juvenile justice programs.

THE ORGANIZATIONAL SYSTEM

Child and Youth Care practice occurs within the context of an agency or organizational system. Skilled practitioners understand the nature of the system and its influence on their practice and work to influence the system so that it offers quality service to all clients. They interpret policy, procedures, and legislation according to the nature of the developmental status of their clients. Professional communication follows but is not limited by the system requirements. The planning and implementation of practice methods take into consideration the nature of the system and its philosophical standpoint. Skilled practitioners integrate the culture of the organization, their own culture, that of their clients, and their co-workers by respecting difference and negotiating a common understanding of right and wrong within this context.

CULTURE

Culture is not just centered in race or ethnicity, but includes the social and political norms, values, morals, faith, language, and socio-economic status of a group of people with a common history. Culture is both a domain of practice and a context within which practice occurs. In the context of culture, skilled practitioners bridge cultural differences through communication and respect for individuals and groups. They actively seek an understanding how culture influences the developmental history of persons and how that may diverge from their own referential framework for culture. Skilled practitioners recognize and adopt a professional culture, without forsaking their own personal culture. In the nexus of culture as a domain of practice and culture as a context for practice, differences are bridged across all other contexts (layers) of practice

Source: Competencies for Professional Child and Youth Work Practitioners 2010. Copyright (c) 2010 Association for Child and Youth Care Practice

Chapter 2 – Let's Reflect

Think of an example where you will use one specific competency in one specific context.

(Remember, in true practice, you likely won't just use one competency at a time and they will overlap and occur in various contexts).

Chapter 2 - Worksheet

Match the competency with the definition

Professionalism	Professional practitioners actively promote respect for cultural and human diversity. The Professional Practitioner seeks self-understanding and has the ability to access and evaluate information related to cultural and human diversity. Current and relevant knowledge is integrated in developing respectful and effective relationships and communication and developmental practice methods. Knowledge and skills are employed in planning, implementing and evaluating respectful programs and services, and workplaces.
Cultural & human diversity	Professional practitioners promote the optimal development of children, youth, and their families in a variety of settings. The developmental-ecological perspective emphasizes the interaction between persons and their physical and social environments, including cultural and political settings. Special attention is given to the everyday lives of children and youth, including those at risk and with special needs, within the family, neighborhood, school and larger social-cultural context. Professional practitioners integrate current knowledge of human development with the skills, expertise, objectivity and self-awareness essential for developing, implementing and evaluating effective programs and services.
Applied human development	Practitioners recognize the critical importance of relationships and communication in the practice of quality child and youth care. Ideally, the service provider and client work in a collaborative manner to achieve growth and change. 'Quality first' practitioners develop genuine relationships based on empathy and positive regard. They are skilled at clear communication, both with clients and with other professionals. Observations and records are objective and respectful of their clients. Relationship and communication are considered in the context of the immediate environment and its conditions; the policy and legislative environment; and the historical and cultural environment of the child, youth or family with which the practitioner interacts.
Relationship & communication	Professional practitioners are generative and flexible; they are self-directed and have a high degree of personal initiative. Their performance is consistently reliable. They function effectively both independently and as a team member. Professional practitioners are knowledgeable about what constitutes a profession, and engage in professional and personal development and self-care. The professional practitioner is aware of the function of professional ethics and uses professional ethics to guide and enhance practice and advocates effectively for children, youth, families, and the profession.
Developmental practice methods	Practitioners recognize the critical importance of developmental practice methods focused in child and youth care practice: Genuine Relationships, Health and Safety, Intervention Planning, Environmental Design and Maintenance, Program Planning and Activity Programming, Activities of Daily Living, Group Work, Counseling, Behavioral Guidance, Family (Caregiver) Engagement, Community Engagement. These are designed to promote optimal development for children, youth, and families including those at-risk and with special needs within the context of the family, community and the lifespan.

Chapter 2 – Checklist

Place a check mark beside the following competencies that you feel you have a complete understanding of. For those not checked, reflect regularly as to how you can develop skills in these areas.

I. Professionalism:

- ☐ Awareness of the profession
- ☐ Professional development and behaviour
- ☐ Personal development and self-care
- ☐ Professional ethics
- ☐ Awareness of law and regulations
- ☐ Advocacy

II. Cultural and Human diversity:

- ☐ Cultural and human diversity awareness inquiry
- ☐ Relationship and communication sensitive to cultural and human diversity
- ☐ Developmental practice methods sensitive to cultural and human diversity

III. Applied Human Development

- ☐ Contextual-developmental assessment
- ☐ Sensitivity to contextual development in relationships and communication
- ☐ Practice methods that are sensitive to development and context
- ☐ Access resources that support healthy development

IV. Relationships & Communication

- ☐ Interpersonal communication
- ☐ Relationship development
- ☐ Family communication
- ☐ Teamwork and professional communication skills

V. Developmental Practice Methods

- ☐ Genuine relationships
- ☐ Health and safety
- ☐ Intervention planning
- ☐ Environmental design and maintenance
- ☐ Program planning and activity programming
- ☐ Activities of daily living
- ☐ Group process
- ☐ Counselling
- ☐ Behaviour guidance
- ☐ Family and caregiver engagement
- ☐ Community engagement

References and Resources

Association for Child and Youth Care Practice. (2010). *Competencies for professional child and youth work practitioners 2010*. ACYCP.

Stuart, Carol. (2010). *Foundations of child and youth care*. Kendall Hund Publishing.

Chapter 3: How Does the Code of Ethics Apply to CYC Practice?

Real Life Story

Review the CYC code of ethics and your agencies code of ethics while considering the following stories:

- A third year CYC student was caught smoking marijuana with some clients while he was actively working at his field placement.
- Group home CYC staff engaging in sexual relationships with clients.
- Group home CYC staff bringing clients to their home and/or providing personal information to clients.
- CYC staff utilizing social media for communication with clients and breaching their confidentiality.
- Respecting client's religious affiliations if applicable (do not force clients to participate in any religious celebrations/ceremonies against their will.
- A foster family was spoken to regarding family members referring to the foster child as, "brown girl".
- A CYC took it upon herself to reorganize a preexisting treatment plan based on experiences she had with her own child.
- Staff sharing answers for mandatory training rather than completing the training thoroughly on their own
- Staff ensuring that we are dressed appropriately for work (court, home visits, group home)

A code of ethics is necessary because it allows individuals to know what is expected of them as acceptable behaviour. It provides guidelines on making decisions that are in line with the goals of the organization.

According to the Life Skills Coaches Association of BC, the purpose of a code of ethics is to:

- define accepted/acceptable behaviours
- promote high standards of practice
- provide a benchmark for members to use for self-evaluation
- establish a framework for professional behaviour and responsibilities
- provide a vehicle for occupational identity
- indicate a level of occupational maturity

Professional Child and Youth Care is committed to promoting the well-being of children, youth, and families in a context of respect and collaboration. This commitment is carried out in a variety of settings and with a broad range of roles including direct practice, supervision, administration, teaching and training, research, consultation, and advocacy. In the course of practice Child and Youth Care Professionals encounter many situations which have ethical dimensions and implications.

As Child and Youth Care Professionals we are aware of, and sensitive to, the responsibilities involved in our practice. Each professional has the responsibility to strive for high standards of professional conduct. This includes a commitment to the centrality of ethical concerns for Child and Youth Care practice, concern with one's own professional conduct, encouraging ethical behaviour by others, and consulting with others on ethical issues.

This ethical statement is a living document, always a work in progress, which will mature and clarify as our understanding and knowledge grow. The principles represent values deeply rooted in our history, to which there is a common commitment. They are intended to serve as guidelines for conduct and to assist in resolving ethical questions. For some dilemmas, the principles provide specific or significant guidance. In other instances, the Child and Youth Care Professional is required to combine the guidance of the principles with sound professional judgment and consultation. In any situation, the course of action chosen is expected to be consistent with the spirit and intent of the principles.

ETHICS OF CHILD AND YOUTH CARE PROFESSIONALS

The following standards of practice are adapted from the Association for Child & Youth Care Practice (www.oacyc.org/code-of-ethics)

PRINCIPLES AND STANDARDS

I. RESPONSIBILITY FOR SELF

A. Maintains competency

    1. Takes responsibility for identifying, developing, and fully utilizing knowledge and abilities for professional practice

    2. Obtains training, education, supervision, experience and/or counsel to assure competent service

B. Maintains high standards of professional conduct

C. Maintains physical and emotional well-being

    1. Aware of own values and their implication for practice

    2. Aware of self as a growing and strengthening professional

II. RESPONSIBILITY TO THE CLIENT

A. Above all, shall not harm the child, youth or family

    1. Does not participate in practices that are disrespectful, degrading, dangerous, exploitive intimidating, psychologically damaging, or physically harmful to clients.

B. Provides expertise and protection

    1. Recognizes, respects, and advocates for the rights of the child, youth and family

C. Recognizes that professional responsibility is to the client and advocates for the client's best interest

> As a Child and Youth Practitioner you will be afforded many opportunities to expand your practice through hands on training, shadowing with co-workers and through clinical supervision. Some of these opportunities will be mandatory and others will be optional.
>
> As the Child and Youth Practitioner field continues to evolve, you should take it upon yourself to explore new and current training opportunities within your organization and outside of your organization. Depending on which organization you work for you might be able to access training opportunities through an online training calendar or you may find out about training opportunities through your Human Resources department.
>
> When we started in the Child Protection field we found that the most beneficial part of our early employment was being able to accompany veteran workers on their home visits with clients. There was no better learning tool than having the ability to see firsthand how a seasoned worker interacted with their clients. We found that our learning experiences were more impactful when we had the chance to observe our coworkers with their clients.
>
>> Clinical supervision focuses on the work that caseworkers do with children and families. Good clinical supervision is critical to building worker competencies, including reinforcing positive social work ethics and values, encouraging self-reflection and critical thinking skills, building upon training to enhance performance, and supporting the worker through casework decision-making and crises. The following resources provide examples of efforts to better understand and enhance the clinical role of supervisors. Clinical Supervision.
>>
>> https://www.childwelfare.gov/topics/management/mgmt-supervision/clinical/

D. Ensures that services are sensitive to and non-discriminatory of clients regardless of race, color, ethnicity, national origin, national ancestry, age, gender, sexual orientation, marital status, religion, abilities, mental or physical handicap, medical condition, political belief, political affiliation, socioeconomic status

   1. Obtains training, education, supervision, experience, and/or counsel to assure competent service

E. Recognizes and respects the expectations and life patterns of clients

   1. Designs individualized programs of child, youth and family care to determine and help meet the psychological, physical, social, cultural and spiritual needs of the clients

   2. Designs programs of child, youth, and family care which address the child's developmental status, understanding, capacity, and age

F. Recognizes that there are differences in the needs of children, youth and families

   1. Meets each client's needs on an individual basis

   2. Considers the implications of acceptance for the child, other children, and the family when gratuities or benefits are offered from a child, youth or family

G. Recognizes that competent service often requires collaboration. Such service is a cooperative effort drawing upon the expertise of many

   1. Administers medication prescribed by the lawful prescribing practitioner in accordance with the prescribed directions and only for medical purposes. Seeks consultation when necessary

2. Refers the client to other professionals and/or seeks assistance to ensure appropriate services

3. Observes, assesses, and evaluates services/treatments prescribed or designed by other professionals

H. Recognizes the client's membership within a family and community, and facilitates the participation of significant others in service to the client

I. Fosters client self-determination

J. Respects the privacy of clients and holds in confidence information obtained in the course of professional service

K. Ensures that the boundaries between professional and personal relationships with clients is explicitly understood and respected, and that the practitioner's behaviour is appropriate to this difference

1. Sexual intimacy with a client, or the family member of a client, is unethical

> First and foremost, we believe that our clients need to be assured that they will be respected and that any information they share with us will be kept confidential. Imagine that you and your family are involved with Child Protection Services. Would you feel ashamed or embarrassed? Our clients are often reluctant to work with us given the reputation that some Child Protection Agencies have within the community. Due to these circumstances it is extremely important for workers to respect the privacy of clients and to treat them with the utmost respect during the working relationship.

III. RESPONSIBILITY TO THE EMPLOYER/EMPLOYING ORGANIZATION

A. Treats colleagues with respect, courtesy, fairness, and good faith

B. Relates to the clients of colleagues with professional consideration

C. Respects the commitments made to the employer/employing organization

IV. RESPONSIBILITY TO THE PROFESSION

A. Recognizes that in situations of professional practice the standards in this code shall guide the resolution of ethical conflicts

B. Promotes ethical conduct by members of the profession

1. Seeks arbitration or mediation when conflicts with colleagues require consultation and if an informal resolution seems appropriate

2. Reports ethical violations to appropriate persons and/or bodies when an informal resolution is not appropriate

C. Encourages collaborative participation by professionals, client, family and community to share responsibility for client outcomes

D. Ensures that research is designed, conducted, and reported in accordance with high quality Child and Youth Care practice, and recognized standards of scholarship, and research ethics

> As a CYC Practitioner you will be required to interact with colleagues, community agencies and other professionals. You will be a valued member of a multi-disciplinary team; you will be developing professional relationships with others in your place of employment, as well as with external agencies, support systems and families. There is an expectation from your employer, clients, society and yourself, that you conduct yourself in a professional manner.
>
> When you first start your job, as a new employee your responsibilities will include learning and understanding your employer's policies and procedures and it will be your job to put these into practice and to abide by them.
>
> When we first started our jobs in child protection there were many procedures and policies that we needed to learn. Not all made sense to us initially, however we recognized that there was a reason for them being put in place.
>
> It is ethically important (and often agency policy) that when interviewing a child alone, that you leave the door to the room you are in, open. This does not necessarily allow for total privacy for the child, however it is a safeguard for yourself, and ultimately the child that will ensure you are not leaving yourself open to allegations of any kind. It is also a safeguard for the child as it provides them with the visual opportunity to leave the room if upset or uncomfortable.

E. Ensures that education and training programs are competently designed and delivered
　1. Programs meet the requirements/claims set forth by the program
　2. Experiences provided are properly supervised

F. Ensures that administrators and supervisors lead programs in high quality and ethical practice in relation to clients, staff, governing
　bodies, and the community

1. Provides support for professional growth

2. Evaluates staff on the basis of performance on established requirements

> Always remember that as a CYC Practitioner, you are not only representing your employer with the work you do, but the Child and Youth Care profession as a whole. This thought should be the underpinning to your behaviours and conduct.
>
> It is almost inevitable that during the course of your employment you will encounter some kind of conflict or difference of opinion with one of your colleagues, community partners or clients. During these time is if of utmost importance that you remain professional, objective and most of all polite.
>
> We have been in conflictual situations with colleagues, where a difference of opinion occurred with regards to the handling of a case. During these times it is critical to keep to the facts of the case and ensure that personal issues are not brought into the conversations. This can be difficult, especially if there is a personality conflict between two colleagues, however for the best interest of the child, you need to maintain your high level of professionalism.

V. RESPONSIBILITY TO SOCIETY

A. Contributes to the profession in making services available to the public

B. Promotes understanding and facilitates acceptance of diversity in society

C. Demonstrates the standards of this Code with students and volunteers

D. Encourages informed participation by the public in shaping social policies and institutions.

As a CYC Practitioner you will likely encounter individuals who do not afford you the respect your education, expertise and skills command. More often than not, this is due to lack of understanding of the profession as opposed to them feeling your contribution is not valuable. As a CYC it is part of your role to educate peers, coworkers, employers and the public sector, to name a few, with regards to your abilities, goals, duties and responsibilities.

Just as a dentist is an expert about teeth, CYC's are experts about their clientele also.

The field should encourage its members to be proactive as opposed to reactive to allow the community to recognize its inherent value.

Any opportunity that you have to support the field and educate the public about it should be undertaken in a professional and enthusiastic manner.

While supporting the values and skills of the CYC practitioner, it is also extremely important to be culturally sensitive and work within an anti-oppressive lens. Your caseload will be very diverse and it is your responsibility to ensure that all your families and clients receive the appropriate plan, attending and respect.

Chapter 3 – Let's Reflect

If you were given the task of updating the existing Code of Ethics for CYC Practitioners, what would you add, delete or expand upon and why?

I would....

Chapter 3 - Worksheet

Real Life Situation	Applicable section from the code of ethics. (there may be more than one)	Why/how does that area of the code of ethics apply to this situation?
A third year CYC student was caught smoking marijuana with some clients while he was actively working at his field placement.		
Group home CYC staff engaging in sexual relationships with clients.		
Group home CYC staff bringing clients to their home and/or providing personal information to clients.		
CYC staff utilizing social media for communication with clients and breaching their confidentiality.		
CYC staff utilizing social media for communication with clients and breaching their confidentiality.		
Respecting client's religious affiliations if applicable (do not force clients to participate in any religious celebrations/ceremonies against their will. A foster family were spoken to regarding family members referring to the foster child as, "brown girl".		
A CYC took it upon herself to reorganize a preexisting treatment plan based on experiences she had with her own child.		
Staff sharing answers for mandatory training rather than completing the training thoroughly on their own (DCAS)		
Staff ensuring that we are dressed appropriately for work (court, home visits, group home) (DCAS)		

Chapter 3 – Checklist

Confirm that you have read and understood the CYC Code of Ethics. Use the checklist below to indicate when you have had the opportunity to utilize each section either in your placement or your employment. (Return to the specific sections to ensure that you understand the subtopic under each section.)

I. Responsibility for Self
- ☐ a. Maintains Competency
- ☐ b. Maintains high standards of professional conduct
- ☐ c. Maintains physical and emotional wellbeing

II. Responsibility to the Client
- ☐ a. Above all, shall not harm the child, youth or family
- ☐ b. Provides expertise and protection
- ☐ c. Recognizes that professional responsibility is to the client and advocates for the client's best interest
- ☐ d. Ensures that services are sensitive to an non-discriminatory of clients, regardless of race, colour, ethnicity, national origin, national ancestry, age, gender, sexual orientation, marital status, religion, abilities, mental or physical handicap, medical condition, political belief, political affiliation, socioeconomic status
- ☐ e. Recognizes and respects the expectations and life patterns of clients
- ☐ f. Recognizes that there are differences in the needs of children, youth and families
- ☐ g. Recognizes that competent service often requires collaboration. Such service is a cooperative effort drawing upon the expertise of many
- ☐ h. Recognizes the client's membership within a family and community, and facilitates the participation of significant other in service to the client
- ☐ i. Fosters client self determination
- ☐ j. Respects the privacy of clients and holds in confidence information obtained in the course of professional service
- ☐ k. Ensures that the boundaries between professional and personal relationships with clients is explicitly understood and respected, and that the practitioner's behaviour is appropriate to this difference

III. Responsibility to the employer/employing organization
- ☐ a. Treats colleagues with respect, courtesy, fairness, and good faith
- ☐ b. Relates to the clients of colleagues with professional consideration
- ☐ c. Respects the commitments made to the employer/employing organization

IV. Responsibility to the Profession
- ☐ a. Recognizes the in situations of professional practice the standards in this code shall guide the resolution of ethical conflicts
- ☐ b. Promotes ethical conduct by members of the profession
- ☐ c. Encourages collaborative participation by professionals, client, family and community to share responsibility for client outcomes

☐ d. Ensures that research is designed, conducted and reported in accordance with high quality Child and Youth Care practice, and recognized standards of scholarship, and research ethics

☐ e. Ensures that education and training programs are competently designed and delivered

☐ f. Ensures that administrators and supervisors lead programs I igh quality and ethical practice in relation to clients, staff, governing bodies, and the community

V. Responsibility to Society

☐ a. Contributes to the profession in making services available to the public

☐ b. Promote understanding and facilitates acceptance of diversity in society

☐ c. Demonstrates the standards of this Code with students and volunteers

☐ d. Encourages informed participation by the public in shaping social policies and institutions

References and Resources

Child Welfare Information Gateway. Retrieved from https://www.childwelfare.gov/topics/management/mgmt-supervision/clinical/

Life Skills Coaches Association of BC.

Martha A. Mattingly, Program in Child Development & Child Care, University of Pittsburgh, Pittsburgh, Pa. 15260, USA

Standards for Practice of North American Child & Youth Care Professionals. (2017). Association for Child & Youth Care Practice. Retrieved from http://www.oacyc.org/about-us/code-of-ethics

Chapter 4: What is the CYFSA and the YCJA and How Does it Imact my Work?

Real Life Story

Depending on the age of the child with whom you are working, there are different sections of the act that apply to them. For example, if a child is under the age of 6 the CFSA mandates that a permanent plan must be made for the child within 1 year of their placement in care. **For children over 6, this timeline is extended to 2 years.**

Therefore, timelines and deadlines are extremely important under the act, and in your practice.

This Real-Life Story occurred while agencies were still legislated by the CFSA, not the updated CYFSA.

While working with a youth who was almost 16 years of age, the timelines were very tight to bring her into care before her 16th birthday to ensure that we had mitigated the risk to the child. However, due to a mix up with changes in workers, the court papers were not filed at the appropriate time, therefore missing the window of opportunity we had with this youth. Due to this, she was beyond the jurisdiction of child welfare and she remained with her family.

Sadly, this youth committed suicide several months later. Now it can't be concluded that the only reason she took her life was due to her family situation, however as a worker I'm sure you cannot help but think that if the paperwork had been filed within the required timelines, we may have been able to protect that child.

Overview of the CYFSA

In 2017, under Bill 89, The Child and Family Service Act (CFSA) underwent changes in response to feedback from a review in 2015 and was named The CYFSA, Child Youth and Family Services Act.

Key changes include:

- Raising the age of protection from 16 to 18 through amendments to the Child and Family Services Act that came into force on January 1, 2018, and will be carried forward in the CYFSA to increase protection services for more vulnerable youth in unsafe living conditions, to support their education and to reduce homelessness and human trafficking;
- Strengthening the focus on early intervention, helping prevent children and families from reaching crisis situations at home;
- Making services more culturally appropriate for all children and youth in the child welfare system, including First Nations, Inuit and Métis and Black children and youth, to help ensure

- they receive the best possible support.
- Improving oversight of service providers, including Children's Aid Societies, so that children and youth receive consistent, high-quality services across Ontario.

The Child Youth and Family Services act is to protect children from harm and to protect the integrity of the family and ensure the best interests of the children.

According to Wegner-Lohin, Kyte, and Trocmé (2014), all Children's Aid Societies in Ontario are mandated under the CYFSA "to protect children who have been or are at risk of being abused and/or neglected by their caregivers, to provide for their care and supervision where necessary and to place children for adoption." In addition to the CYFSA, the Ontario Child Welfare Eligibility Spectrum and Child Protection Standards guide child protection workers at each phase of service delivery.

Indian Bands (that operate under the Indian Act) are accountable to the communities they serve.

In order for a child to be found in need of protection, evidence of harm is not required. Children can be deemed as being in need of protection when there is a risk that the child is likely to be sexually molested or exploited, suffer physical harm, or emotional harm (www.cwrp.ca)

> When child abuse or neglect is suspected, the information is reported to the local Children's Aid Society. Each report of a child protection concern is assessed by a child protection worker based on the Child Protection Standards in Ontario and the Eligibility Spectrum. In cases where there are reasonable and probable grounds that a child may be in need of protection, an investigation is initiated using either a "traditional approach" (focused on ascertaining facts and collecting evidence in a legally defensible manner) or a "customized approach" (more flexible, individualized approach used in less severe cases).
>
> Wegner-Lohin, Kyte, and Trocmé (2014)

Primary Category of Substantiated Maltreatment in Ontario, 2008

Primary Category	Percentage	Number of Substantiated Maltreatment Investigations
Neglect	46%	2,781
Exposure to domestic violence	33%	2,000
Physical abuse	9%	560
Emotional maltreatment	9%	559
Sexual abuse	2%	292

Source: Sinha, V., Trocmé, N., Fallon, B., MacLaurin, B., Fast, E., Thomas Prokop, S., ... Richard, K. (2011). *Kiskisik Awasisak: Remember the Children. Understanding the Overrepresentation of First Nations Children in the Child Welfare System*. Ontario: Assembly of First Nations.

AS a CYC Practitioner you should be familiar with the CYFSA, you likely will not be required to memorize the act, however, there will be certain sections that will be more applicable to your work than others.

If you pursue a career path in child protection, you will be exposed to the CYFSA on an ongoing basis. However, if you choose a career outside of direct child protection, you will also have exposure to the CYFSA throughout your career.

Paramount to any work you do with children and youth will be the Rights of Children and Young Person's receiving service. This will be the baseline for your practice.

Rights of children, young persons receiving services

Every child and young person receiving services under this Act has the following rights:

- To express their own views freely and safely about matters that affect them.
- To be engaged through an honest and respectful dialogue about how and why decisions affecting them are made and to have their views given due weight, in accordance with their age and maturity.
- To be consulted on the nature of the services provided or to be provided to them, to participate in decisions about the services provided or to be provided to them and to be advised of the decisions made in respect of those services.
- To raise concerns or recommend changes with respect to the services provided or to be provided to them without interference or fear of coercion, discrimination or reprisal and to receive a response to their concerns or recommended changes.
- To be informed, in language suitable to their understanding, of their rights under this Part.

> Repealed: 2018, c. 17, Sched. 34, s. 6 (1). Sections 8(1); 10(1); further discuss the rights of the child.

Keep in mind, that these rights, are specific to the rights of a child receiving services under the Act, however, this does not preclude the rights of the child as governed by the UN, which can be found at: https://www.ohchr.org/en/professionalinterest/pages/crc.aspx.

Children and Youth Entering Care

Your role as a CYC in a child protection setting begins once a child has been deemed in need of protection under Section 74.2 of the CYFSA and has been placed in interim society care (CYFSA Sec. 101.2). Once a child enters into the care of a Society, you, as a CYC will be responsible for their care and well-being.

At this point, a placement option has already been established for the child, which could include, foster home, kin in care home, customary care or a group home setting. Depending on the needs of the child/youth it could also include secure custody or a mental health placement.

The definition of a child in need of protection, according to the Act is as follows:

Definition

Child in need of protection

(2) A child is in need of protection where,

> (a) the child has suffered physical harm, inflicted by the person having charge of the child or caused by or resulting from that person's,

(i) failure to adequately care for, provide for, supervise or protect the child, or

(ii) pattern of neglect in caring for, providing for, supervising or protecting the child;

(b) there is a risk that the child is likely to suffer physical harm inflicted by the person having charge of the child or caused by or resulting from that person's,

(i) failure to adequately care for, provide for, supervise or protect the child, or

(ii) pattern of neglect in caring for, providing for, supervising or protecting the child;

(c) the child has been sexually abused or sexually exploited, by the person having charge of the child or by another person where the person having charge of the child knows or should know of the possibility of sexual abuse or sexual exploitation and fails to protect the child;

(d) there is a risk that the child is likely to be sexually abused or sexually exploited as described in clause (c);

(e) the child requires treatment to cure, prevent or alleviate physical harm or suffering and the child's parent or the person having charge of the child does not provide the treatment or access to the treatment, or, where the child is incapable of consenting to the treatment under the _Health Care Consent Act, 1996_ and the parent is a substitute decision-maker for the child, the parent refuses or is unavailable or unable to consent to the treatment on the child's behalf;

(f) the child has suffered emotional harm, demonstrated by serious,

(i) anxiety,

(ii) depression,

(iii) withdrawal,

(iv) self-destructive or aggressive behaviour, or

(v) delayed development, and there are reasonable grounds to believe that the emotional harm suffered by the child results from the actions, failure to act or pattern of neglect on the part of the child's parent or the person having charge of the child;

(g) the child has suffered emotional harm of the kind described in subclause (f) (i), (ii), (iii), (iv) or (v) and the child's parent or the person having charge of the child does not provide services or treatment or access to services or treatment, or, where the child is incapable of consenting to treatment under the _Health Care Consent Act, 1996_, refuses or is unavailable or unable to consent to the treatment to remedy or alleviate the harm;

(h) there is a risk that the child is likely to suffer emotional harm of the kind described in subclause (f) (i), (ii), (iii), (iv) or (v) resulting from the actions, failure to act or pattern of neglect on the part of the child's parent or the person having charge of the child;

(i) there is a risk that the child is likely to suffer emotional harm of the kind described in subclause (f) (i), (ii), (iii), (iv) or (v) and that the child's parent or the person having charge of the child does not provide services or treatment or access to services or treatment, or, where the child is incapable of consenting to treatment under the _Health Care Consent Act, 1996_, refuses or is unavailable or unable to consent to treatment to prevent the harm;

(j) the child suffers from a mental, emotional or developmental condition that, if not remedied, could seriously impair the child's development and the child's parent or the person having charge of the child does not provide treatment or access to treatment, or where the child is incapable of consenting to treatment under the _Health Care Consent Act, 1996_, refuses or is unavailable or unable to consent to the treatment to remedy or alleviate the condition;

(k) the child's parent has died or is unavailable to exercise custodial rights over the child and has not made adequate provision for the child's care and custody, or the child is in a residential placement and the parent refuses or is unable or unwilling to resume the child's care and custody;

(l) the child is younger than 12 and has killed or seriously injured another person or caused serious damage to another person's property, services or treatment are necessary to prevent a recurrence and the child's parent or the person having charge of the child does not provide services or treatment or access to services or treatment, or, where the child is incapable of consenting to treatment under the _Health Care Consent Act, 1996_, refuses or is unavailable or unable to consent to treatment;

(m) the child is younger than 12 and has on more than one occasion injured another person or caused loss or damage to another person's property, with the encouragement of the person having charge of the child or because of that person's failure or inability to supervise the child adequately;

(n) the child's parent is unable to care for the child and the child is brought before the court with the parent's consent and, where the child is 12 or older, with the child's consent, for the matter to be dealt with under this Part; or

(o) the child is 16 or 17 and a prescribed circumstance or condition exists.

Order where child in need of protection

101 (1) Where the court finds that a child is in need of protection and is satisfied that intervention through a court order is necessary to protect the child in the future, the court shall make one of the following orders or an order under section 102, in the child's best interests:

Supervision order

1. That the child be placed in the care and custody of a parent or another person, subject to the supervision of the society, for a specified period of at least three months and not more than 12 months.

Interim society care

2. That the child be placed in interim society care and custody for a specified period not exceeding 12 months.

Extended society care

3. That the child be placed in extended society care until the order is terminated under section 116 or expires under section 123.

Consecutive orders of interim society care and supervision

4. That the child be placed in interim society care and custody under paragraph 2 for a specified period and then be returned to a parent or another person under paragraph 1, for a period or periods not exceeding a total of 12 months.

Customary care

80 A society shall make all reasonable efforts to pursue a plan for customary care for a First Nations, Inuk or Métis child if the child,

(a) is in need of protection;

(b) cannot remain in or be returned to the care and custody of the person who had charge of the child immediately before intervention under this Part or, where there is an order for the child's custody that is enforceable in Ontario, of the person entitled to custody under the order; and

(c) is a member of or identifies with a band, or is a member of or identifies with a First Nations, Inuit or Métis community.

Best interests of child

(3) Where a person is directed in this Part to make an order or determination in the best interests of a child, the person shall,

(a) consider the child's views and wishes, given due weight in accordance with the child's age and maturity, unless they cannot be ascertained;

(b) in the case of a First Nations, Inuk or Métis child, consider the importance, in recognition of the uniqueness of First Nations, Inuit and Métis cultures, heritages and traditions, of preserving the child's cultural identity and connection to community, in addition to the considerations under clauses (a) and (c); and

(c) consider any other circumstance of the case that the person considers relevant, including,

(i) the child's physical, mental and emotional needs, and the appropriate care or treatment to meet those needs,

(ii) the child's physical, mental and emotional level of development,

(iii) the child's race, ancestry, place of origin, colour, ethnic origin, citizenship, family diversity, disability, creed, sex, sexual orientation, gender identity and gender expression,

(iv) the child's cultural and linguistic heritage,

(v) the importance for the child's development of a positive relationship with a parent and a secure place as a member of a family,

(vi) the child's relationships and emotional ties to a parent, sibling, relative, other member of the child's extended family or member of the child's community,

(vii) the importance of continuity in the child's care and the possible effect on the child of disruption of that continuity,

(viii) the merits of a plan for the child's care proposed by a society, including a proposal that the child be placed for adoption or adopted, compared with the merits of the child remaining with or returning to a parent,

(ix) the effects on the child of delay in the disposition of the case,

(x) the risk that the child may suffer harm through being removed from, kept away from, returned to or allowed to remain in the care of a parent, and

(xi) the degree of risk, if any, that justified the finding that the child is in need of protection.

During your ongoing interaction with children/youth on your caseload you will be required to ensure your clients are aware of their rights and responsibilities. These differ depending on the age of the child and the setting in which they are placed.

Plans of Care & Rights of the Child

Within the first 30 days of a child entering into care, the child has a right to a Plan of Care, which is designed to meet his or her particular needs (CYFSA Sec. 13 (1)).

Plan of care

13 (1) A child in care has a right to a plan of care designed to meet their particular needs, which shall be prepared within 30 days of the child's or young person's admission to the residential placement.

Rights to care

(2) A child in care has a right,

- (a) to participate in the development of their individual plan of care and in any changes made to it;
- (b) to have access to food that is of good quality and appropriate for the child or young person, including meals that are well balanced;
- (c) to be provided with clothing that is of good quality and appropriate for the child or young person, given their size and activities and prevailing weather conditions;
- (d) to receive medical and dental care, subject to section 14, at regular intervals and whenever required, in a community setting whenever possible;
- (e) to receive an education that corresponds to their aptitudes and abilities, in a community setting whenever possible; and
- (f) to participate in recreational, athletic and creative activities that are appropriate for their aptitudes and interests, in a community setting whenever possible.

Duty to Report

While in care and on your caseload, the child/youth could disclose concerns surrounding current or historical abuse/trauma/neglect or other child protection issues to you. As a professional you have the legal and moral obligation to report this information to the appropriate people.

Duty to report child in need of protection

125 (1) Despite the provisions of any other Act, if a person, including a person who performs professional or official duties with respect to children, has reasonable grounds to suspect one of the following, the person shall immediately report the suspicion and the information on which it is based to a society:

1. The child has suffered physical harm inflicted by the person having charge of the child or caused by or resulting from that person's,

    i. failure to adequately care for, provide for, supervise or protect the child, or

    ii. pattern of neglect in caring for, providing for, supervising or protecting the child.

2. There is a risk that the child is likely to suffer physical harm inflicted by the person having charge of the child or caused by or resulting from that person's,

    i. failure to adequately care for, provide for, supervise or protect the child, or

    ii. pattern of neglect in caring for, providing for, supervising or protecting the child.

3. The child has been sexually abused or sexually exploited by the person having charge of the child or by another person where the person having charge of the child knows or should know of the possibility of sexual abuse or sexual exploitation and fails to protect the child.

4. There is a risk that the child is likely to be sexually abused or sexually exploited as described in paragraph 3.

5. The child requires treatment to cure, prevent or alleviate physical harm or suffering and the child's parent or the person having charge of the child does not provide the treatment or access to the treatment, or, where the child is incapable of consenting to the treatment under the Health Care Consent Act, 1996, refuses or is unavailable or unable to consent to, the treatment on the child's behalf.

6. The child has suffered emotional harm, demonstrated by serious,

    i. anxiety,

    ii. depression,

    iii. withdrawal,

    iv. self-destructive or aggressive behaviour, or

    v. delayed development, and there are reasonable grounds to believe that the emotional harm suffered by the child results from the actions, failure to act or pattern of neglect on the part of the child's parent or the person having charge of the child.

7. The child has suffered emotional harm of the kind described in subparagraph 6 i, ii, iii, iv or v and the child's parent or the person having charge of the child does not provide services or treatment or access to services or treatment, or, where the child is incapable of consenting to treatment under the Health Care Consent Act, 1996, refuses or is unavailable or unable to consent to, treatment to remedy or alleviate the harm.

8. There is a risk that the child is likely to suffer emotional harm of the kind described in subparagraph 6 i, ii, iii, iv or v resulting from the actions, failure to act or pattern of neglect on the part of the child's parent or the person having charge of the child.

9. There is a risk that the child is likely to suffer emotional harm of the kind described in subparagraph 6 i, ii, iii, iv or v and the child's parent or the person having charge of the child does not provide services or treatment or access to services or treatment, or, where the child is incapable of consenting to treatment under the Health Care Consent Act, 1996, refuses or is unavailable or unable to consent to, treatment to prevent the harm.

10. The child suffers from a mental, emotional or developmental condition that, if not remedied, could seriously impair the child's development and the child's parent or the person having charge of the child does not provide the treatment or access to the treatment, or where the child is incapable of consenting to the treatment under the Health Care Consent Act, 1996, refuses or is unavailable or unable to consent to, treatment to remedy or alleviate the condition.

11. The child's parent has died or is unavailable to exercise custodial rights over the child and has not made adequate provision for the child's care and custody, or the child is in a residential placement and the parent refuses or is unable or unwilling to resume the child's care and custody.

12. The child is younger than 12 and has killed or seriously injured another person or caused serious damage to another person's property, services or treatment are necessary to prevent a recurrence and the child's parent or the person having charge of the child does not provide services or treatment or access to services or treatment, or, where the child is incapable of consenting to treatment under the Health Care Consent Act, 1996, refuses or is unavailable or unable to consent to treatment.

13. The child is younger than 12 and has on more than one occasion injured another person or caused loss or damage to another person's property, with the encouragement of the person having charge of the child or because of that person's failure or inability to supervise the child adequately.

Access

To maintain family relationships and connections with biological family, it has been determined that access with family members can be beneficial if it is in the best interest of the child (C.FSA Sec. 104).

Access can occur in a supervised environment that is determined safe by child protection standards. As a CYC you might be responsible for facilitating and/or supervising these visits. You will be entrusted with the task of ensuring that the contact between the caregiver and the child/youth is appropriate and positive where all members are engaged in rebuilding the relationship.

Throughout the life of your file within a child welfare agency, you will be responsible for monthly visits and annual ONLAC (Ontario Looking After Children) plans of care. If you are not directly within a child protection agency your input into these meetings and plans of care will e invaluable to the therapeutic multi-disciplinary team.

Psychotropic Drugs

At some point in time in your practice as a CYC you will have a child on your caseload that will require the administration of ongoing medications for various issues.

According to MeicineNet a psychotropic drug is "any medication capable of affecting the mind, emotions, and behaviour. Some medications such as lithium, which may be used to treat depression, are psychotropic."

While working with a child on your caseload or a child residing in your place of employment, you will be required to secure the appropriate consents from the applicable persons for the administration of medication to that child or youth.

Below you will find section 132 of the CFSA that outlines the information surrounding the consents required for the use of psychotropic drugs. Ensure that you familiarize yourself with this section.

Consent required for use of psychotropic drugs

176 A service provider shall not administer or permit the administration of a psychotropic drug to a child or young person in the service provider's care without a consent in accordance with the Health Care Consent Act, 1996.

Runaways

Often when children and youth are placed in care they are upset, angry, sad and lonely. They are not happy about their life circumstances and are frustrated by the loss of control. Because of these reasons and other life circumstances, youth may run from their placement and be deemed AWOL, meaning absent without leave or permission.

As the legal guardian for the child, the CYC within the child protection agency should be alerted and will be required to locate and return the youth to their place of care. This is not always the easiest task and may require searching over several days, contacting the youth's friends, family and/or school. It will also require the CYC practitioner to obtain a warrant to apprehend a runaway child as outlined in Section 83 of the CYFSA. If you are a CYC practitioner working in a setting other than Child Protection, you also have the responsibility to contact the youth's legal guardian and advise them of their status.

83. (1) In this section, "parent" includes,

(a) an approved agency that has custody of the child,

(b) a person who has care and control of the child.

Warrant to apprehend runaway child

Bringing children who are removed from or leave care to a place of safety

With warrant

83 (1) A justice of the peace may issue a warrant authorizing a child protection worker to bring a child to a place of safety if the justice of the peace is satisfied on the basis of a child protection worker's sworn information that,

   (a) the child is actually or apparently younger than 16, and,

      (i) has left or been removed from a society's lawful care and custody without its consent, or

      (ii) is the subject of an extra-provincial child protection order and has left or been removed from the lawful care and custody of the child welfare authority or other person named in the order; and

   (b) there are reasonable and probable grounds to believe that there is no course of action available other than bringing the child to a place of safety that would adequately protect the child.

Notice to parent, etc.

84(2) The person in charge of a place of safety to which a child is taken under subsection (3) shall make reasonable efforts to notify the child's parent that the child is in the place of safety so that the child may be returned to the parent.

Interim and Extended Society Care

Section 109 of the Child, Youth and Family Services Act addresses children who are in the care of a Children's Aid Society that are either in interim or extended society care.

Interim Society Care: Interim Society Care previously referred to as Society Wardship, is when the CAS has temporary custody of a child. While the CAS has main responsibility for the child's care, the CAS is still required to keep the parent(s) informed about the child's health and well-being and must also involve the parent(s) in decision making about the child.

Extended Society Care: Extended Society Care previously referred to as Crown Wardship means the CAS has been given custody of the child by the court. With a child under 6, the Crown Wardship order often says there is no access to the parent(s) so the child can be placed for adoption. With older children, the order can allow access to the parent(s) (www.georgehullcentre.on.ca)

Placement of children

109 (1) This section applies where a child is in interim society care under an order made under paragraph 2 of subsection 101 (1) or extended society care under an order made under paragraph 3 of subsection 101 (1) or clause 116 (1) (c).

Placement

(2) The society having care of a child shall choose a residential placement for the child that,

   (a) represents the least restrictive alternative for the child;

   (b) where possible, respects the child's race, ancestry, place of origin, colour, ethnic origin, citizenship, family diversity, creed, sex, sexual orientation, gender identity and gender expression;

(c) where possible, respects the child's cultural and linguistic heritage;

(d) in the case of a First Nations, Inuk or Métis child, is with, if possible, a member of the child's extended family or, if that is not possible,

(i) in the case of a First Nations child, another First Nations family,

(ii) in the case of an Inuk child, another Inuit family, or

(iii) in the case of a Métis child, another Métis family; and

(e) takes into account the child's views and wishes, given due weight in accordance with the child's age and maturity, and the views and wishes of any parent who is entitled to access to the child.

Education

(3) The society having care of a child shall ensure that the child receives an education that corresponds to the child's aptitudes and abilities.

Placement outside or removal from Ontario

(4) The society having care of a child shall not place the child outside Ontario or permit a person to remove the child from Ontario permanently unless a Director is satisfied that extraordinary circumstances justify the placement or removal.

Rights of child, parent and foster parent

(5) The society having care of a child shall ensure that,

(a) the child is afforded all the rights referred to in Part II (Children's and Young Persons' Rights); and

(b) the wishes of any parent who is entitled to access to the child and, where the child is in extended society care under an order made under paragraph 3 of subsection 101 (1) or clause 116 (1) (c), of any foster parent with whom the child has lived continuously for two years are taken into account in the society's major decisions concerning the child.

Change of placement

(6) The society having care of a child may remove the child from a foster home or other residential placement where, in the opinion of a Director or local director, it is in the child's best interests to do so.

Notice of proposed removal

(7) If a child is in extended society care under an order made under paragraph 3 of subsection 101 (1) or clause 116 (1) (c) and has lived continuously with a foster parent for two years and a society proposes to remove the child from the foster parent under subsection (6), the society shall,

(a) give the foster parent at least 10 days notice in writing of the proposed removal and of the foster parent's right to apply for a review under subsection (8); and

(b) in the case of a First Nations, Inuk or Métis child, give the notice required by clause (a), and

(i) give at least 10 days notice in writing of the proposed removal to a representative chosen by each of the child's bands and First Nations, Inuit or Métis communities, and

(ii) after the notice is given under subclause (i), consult with representatives chosen by the bands and communities relating to the plan of care for the child.

VYSA Voluntary Youth Services Agreement

Historically, children in need of protection under the age of 16 fell under the jurisdiction of child protective services. On January 1st, 2018 Ontario increased the age of protection to include all children under the age of 18 years. If a youth is 16 or 17 years old and believes they might be in need of protection due to physical abuse, sexual abuse, neglect and/or abandonment, of if the are at risk of any of these things, they may be eligible for services from a Children's Aid Society.

If a youth has left home or is homeless and feel they may be in need of protection this program could be of benefit to them.

Increasing the age of protection means that youth may be eligible to enter into a new Voluntary Youth Services Agreement (VYSA) if you:

- are aged 16 or 17;
- cannot be adequately protected at home or in your current living situation;
- have no other safe options with family, friends or other member of your community or extended family; and
- need an out-of-home placement.

As a CYC practitioner, what can you tell youth you are working with about VYSA? The Ministry of Children, Community and Youth Services provides information regarding Protection Services for youth, 16-17 years old. This is a new addition to the previous legislation that allows children/youth over the age of 16, supports if they feel they are in need of protection.

There are many facets of the CYFSA that we have not touched upon in this section of the text. You will not need to memorize all the sections of the act however; you will need to be aware of the sections that do apply to your work as a CYC practitioner. We have tried to highlight the main sections that will directly apply to your work.

Services available for 16- and 17-year-olds include (www.children.gov.on.ca):

- Where appropriate, societies will work with you and your family (or if you aren't living with your family, in your current living situation) to improve things at home. This may include referring you and/or your family to community services and programs that can help.

- If you are not safe at home or have left home because you were unsafe, there may be a member of your family or someone close to you who is willing to help. If you can be cared for by members of your family, community or friends, this is called **Kinship Service**.

- If you are a First Nation, Inuk, or Métis youth who needs an out of home placement, a placement can be arranged for your care according to the custom of your band or First Nation, Métis, or Inuit community. This is called **Customary Care**.

- If you are in need of protection, and you cannot be adequately protected at home or in your current living situation, and there are no safe options with family or friends, you may enter into an agreement with a society for services and supports, including a housing option that is safe and appropriate. This is called a **Voluntary Youth Services Agreement (VYSA)**.

- If you are 16- or 17-years old and you are in need of protection, a society will support you to make decisions that help to minimize the risk to your safety and promote your best interests, protection and well-being.

You should expect to be involved in all important decisions that concern you. This includes:

- the plan for your safety;
- your living arrangement;
- your interests regarding education or employment;
- medical care; and
- any programs that will support you in your transition to adulthood.

When you receive services from a society, you should expect support in identifying and developing relationships that you feel are important and beneficial to you, and that you want to last throughout your life. Maintaining healthy family, friend and kinship relationships has proven to be beneficial for children and youth. Services will focus on helping you stay connected to your family – whatever that means to you – and to your community and culture. You should have access to services and supports that respect your culture, as well as access to programs that help you develop personally.

What is a Voluntary Youth Services Agreement (VYSA)?

You can enter an agreement with a society where you reside to receive services and supports, subject to the following eligibility criteria, which are all required:

- the society has determined that you are or may be in need of protection;
- the society has determined that you cannot be adequately protected through any other means such as being cared for by a family member or someone in your community; and
- you want to enter into the agreement.

When you enter a VYSA, you are eligible for a number of supports which may include living arrangements, financial and social supports. The society will work with you to develop a Voluntary Youth Services (VYS) Plan that will outline the different supports available to you.

Prior to entering a VYSA, societies will:

- ensure you meet eligibility requirements;
- inform you of the voluntary nature of the agreement in a manner that you can understand;
- make a referral to the Office of the Children's Lawyer to provide you with an opportunity to receive legal advice about the options available to you; and
- provide you with an opportunity to consult with an advocate or trusted adult prior to signing the agreement and/or have these persons attend planning meetings with you.

If you are a First Nation, Inuk, or Métis youth, the society will provide notice to your First Nation band, or First Nation, Métis, or Inuit community, that the society is preparing to enter an agreement with you so that services are provided to you in a manner that respects and helps preserve your cultural identity and supports you to remain connected to your community, heritage and traditions.

Voluntary Youth Service Plan (VYS Plan)

Every youth who enters a VYSA will have a VYS Plan. This is a plan developed by you and the society that will outline the different supports available to you. It will also document your strengths, needs and goals. It also includes the activities, and assigned roles and responsibilities of you and the society to build on your strengths and respond to your needs and goals. Within 30 days of entering a VYSA, the society worker will work with you to develop a VYS Plan.

What happens when you turn 18?

If you have a VYSA in place with a society on your 18th birthday, you are eligible for the Continued Care and Support for Youth (CCSY) program. CCSY provides eligible youth with financial and non-financial supports (e.g. service from a society worker) from age 18 until your 21st birthday. Talk to your society worker about the range of supports that may be available to you.

Source: www.children.gov.on.ca

Overview of the Youth Criminal Justice Act

Youth Criminal Justice Act

The **Youth Criminal Justice Act** is the law that governs Canada's youth justice system. It applies to youth who are at least 12 but under 18 years old, who are alleged to have committed criminal offences (www.justice.gc.ca).

The Youth Criminal Justice Act came into force in 2003. At that time, it completely replaced the Juvenile Delinquents Act (1908-1984), and the Young Offenders Act (YOA) (1984-2003).

The YCJA reserves the most serious interventions for the most serious crimes and reduces the over-reliance on incarceration for nonviolent young offenders.

Structure of the YCJA:

Part 1: Extrajudicial measure

This section refers to any measures that are an alternative to traditional court proceedings. They can include pre-charge diversions and possibly the administration of police or Crown "Cautions" and referrals to mental health facilities. Sanctions usually include community service.

Part 2: Organization

A youth justice court has exclusive jurisdiction in respect of any offence alleged to have been committed by a person while he or she was a young person.

A "young person" is defined as any person who is between the ages of 12 and 17 or who in the absence of evidence, appears to be within those ages. It includes any offender charged at age 21 if he or she committed the offence while under the age of 18.

Trial by Jury

Trial by jury means that for any indictable offenses youth in trouble with the law are, like adults, entitled to a trial by jury. For summary offenses the youth does not have the right to trial by jury.

Part 3: Judicial Measures

Allows the attorney general to establish a "program of pre-charge screening" that would establish a consent basis for prosecutions in the jurisdiction to which the program applies

The YCJA contains both a Preamble and a Declaration of Principle that applies throughout the Act. The Preamble contains significant statements from Parliament about the values upon which the legislation is based. These statements can be used to help interpret the legislation and include the following:

- Society has a responsibility to address the developmental challenges and needs of young persons.
- Communities and families should work in partnership with others to prevent youth crime by addressing its underlying causes, responding to the needs of young persons and providing guidance and support.
- Accurate information about youth crime, the youth justice system and effective measures should be publicly available.
- Young persons have special guarantees of their rights and freedoms, including those set out in the United Nations Convention on the Rights of the Child.
- The youth justice system should take into account the interests of victims and ensure accountability through meaningful consequences, rehabilitation and reintegration.
- The youth justice system should reserve its most serious interventions for the most serious crimes and reduce the over-reliance on incarceration.

The Declaration of Principle sets out the policy framework of the legislation. Unlike previous youth justice legislation, the YCJA provides guidance on the priority that is to be given to key principles.

The Declaration of Principle provides that:

- The youth justice system is intended to protect the public by (i) holding young persons accountable through measures that are proportionate to the seriousness of the offence and the degree of responsibility of the young person, (ii) promoting the rehabilitation and reintegration of young persons, and (iii) supporting crime prevention by referring young persons to programs or agencies in the community to address the circumstances underlying their offending behaviour.
- The youth justice system must be separate from the adult system and must be based on the principle of diminished moral blameworthiness or culpability.
- The youth justice system must reflect the fact that young people lack the maturity of adults. The youth system is different from the adult system in many respects: measures of accountability are consistent with young persons' reduced level of maturity, procedural protections are enhanced, rehabilitation and reintegration are given special emphasis, and the importance of timely intervention is recognized.

- Young persons are to be held accountable through interventions that are fair and in proportion to the seriousness of the offence.
- Within the limits of fair and proportionate accountability, interventions should reinforce respect for societal values; encourage the repair of harm done; be meaningful to the young person; respect gender, ethnic, cultural and linguistic differences; and respond to the needs of Aboriginal young persons and young persons with special requirements.
- Youth justice proceedings require a recognition that young persons have rights and freedoms in their own right and special guarantees of these rights and freedoms; courtesy, compassion and respect for victims; the opportunity for victims to be informed and to participate; and that parents be informed and encouraged to participate in addressing the young person's offending behaviour.

Due to the significant changes between the Young Offenders Act and the Youth Criminal Justice Act, the percentage of charges laid and the number of youth court cases, decreased significantly between 1999 and 2010.

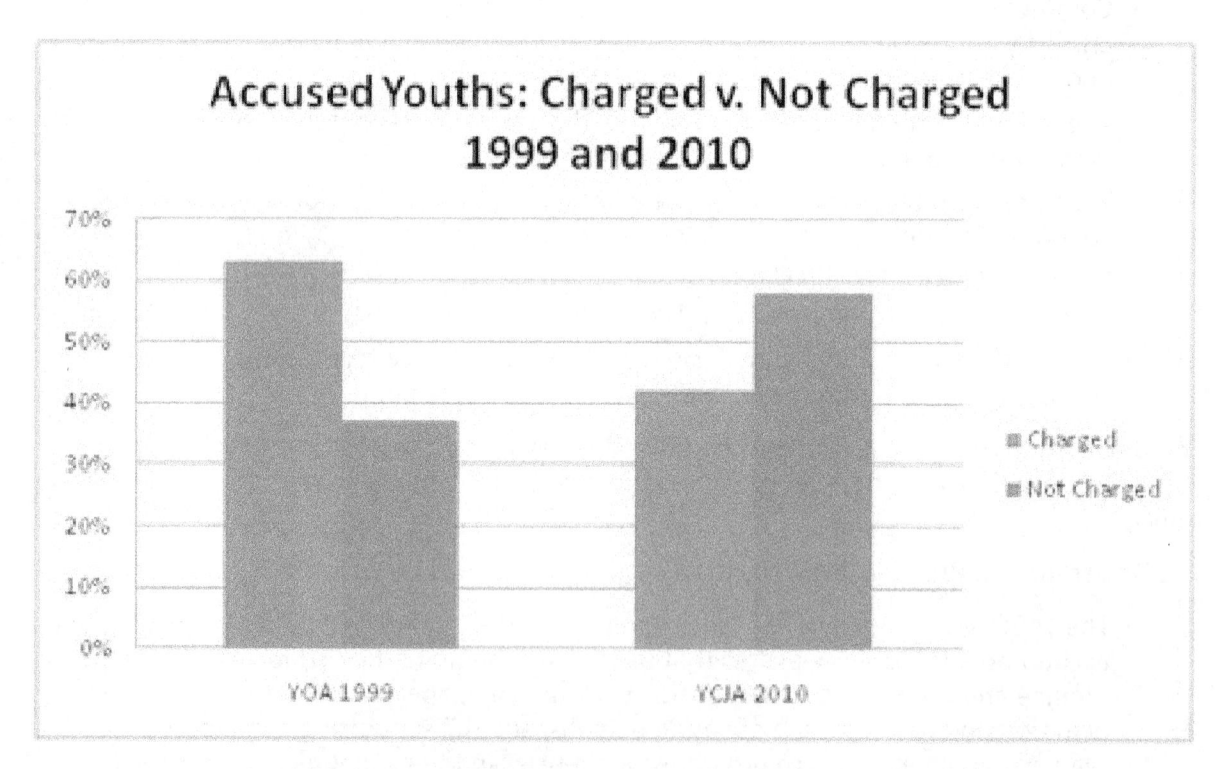

Accused Youths: Charged v. Not Charged 1999 and 2010

	Charged	Not Charged
YOA 1999	~63%	~37%
YCJA 2010	~42%	~58%

Source: Canadian Centre for Justice Statistics, Youth Court Survey

The main changes that led to the YCJA are as follows:

Declaration of principle

- Under the YCJA, the purpose of youth sentences is to hold young persons accountable through just sanctions that ensure meaningful consequences for them and promote their rehabilitation and reintegration into society, thereby contributing to the long-term protection of the public.

Youth Court Cases, Canada 2002/03 - 2009/10

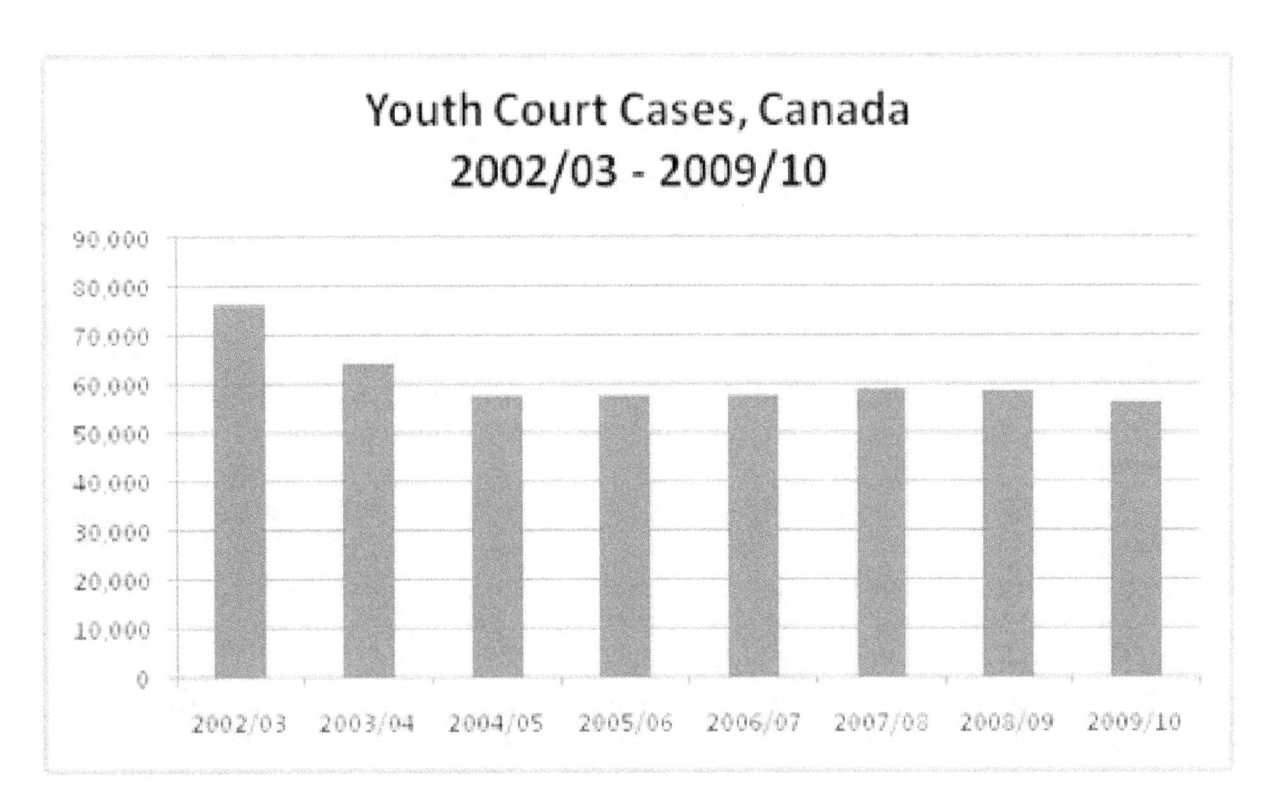

Source: Canadian Centre for Justice Statistics, Youth Court Survey

---

- Provides a clear statement of goal and principles underlying the Act and youth justice system.
- Includes specific principles to guide the use of extrajudicial measures, the imposition of a sentence and custody.

Measures outside the court process

- Creates a presumption that measures other than court proceedings should be used for a first, non-violent offence.
- Encourages their use in all cases where they are sufficient to hold a young person accountable.
- Encourages the involvement of families, victims and community members.

Youth sentences

- Under the YCJA, custody sentences are intended to be reserved primarily for violent offenders and serious repeat offenders.
- In general, the sentencing options that were available to the court under the YOA, such as probation or community service, were retained in the YCJA. However, the YCJA contains significant improvements regarding youth sentencing options.
- The YCJA replaced the usual custody order with a custody and supervision order. This sentence is composed of a portion in custody and a portion in the community.

    Sentencing principles:

    - Includes specific principles, including need for proportionate sentences and importance of rehabilitation.

Sentencing Options:

- Custody reserved for violent or repeat offences.
- All custody sentences to be followed with a period of supervision in the community.
- New options added to encourage use of non-custody sentences and support reintegration.
- Creation of intensive custody and supervision order for serious violent offenders.

Adult sentences

- For nearly 100 years prior to the YCJA, Canada's youth justice legislation allowed young persons who were 14 years of age or older to be transferred to adult court under certain circumstances. If the young person was convicted in adult court, the court imposed an adult sentence.
- Youth justice court empowered to impose an adult sentence, eliminating transfer to adult court.
- Age limit for presumption of adult sentences for the most serious offences is lowered to 14 (however, provinces will have increased flexibility in regard to the age at which this presumption will apply within their jurisdiction).
- The most serious offences that carry a presumption of an adult sentence are extended to include pattern of serious, repeat, violent offences.
- The Crown can renounce the application of the presumption of adult sentence. In this case, the judge who finds the young person guilty has to impose a youth sentence.

Publication

- Permitted if an adult sentence is imposed; or if a youth sentence is imposed for an offence that carries a presumption of adult sentence, unless the judge decides publication is inappropriate.
- Permitted only after the young person has been found guilty.
- Concerns of victims are recognized in principles of the Act.

Victims

- Victims have right to access youth court records and may be given access to other records.
- Role in formal and informal community-based measures is encouraged.
- Establishes right of victims to information on extrajudicial measures taken.

Voluntary statements to police

- Can be admitted into evidence, despite minor, technical irregularities in complying with the statutory protections for young persons.

Advisory groups (conferences)

- Allows advisory groups or "conferences" to advise police officer, judge or other decision-maker under the Act.
- They can advise on appropriate extrajudicial measures, conditions for release from pretrial detention, appropriate sentences and reintegration plans.
- Conferences may include parents of the young person, victim, community agencies or professionals.

Custody and reintegration

- All custody sentences comprise a portion served in custody and a portion served under supervision in the community.
- A plan for reintegration in the community must be prepared for each youth in custody.
- Reintegration leaves may be granted for up to 30 days.

Source: http://www.newlearner.com/courses/hts/cln4u/blwho90.htm

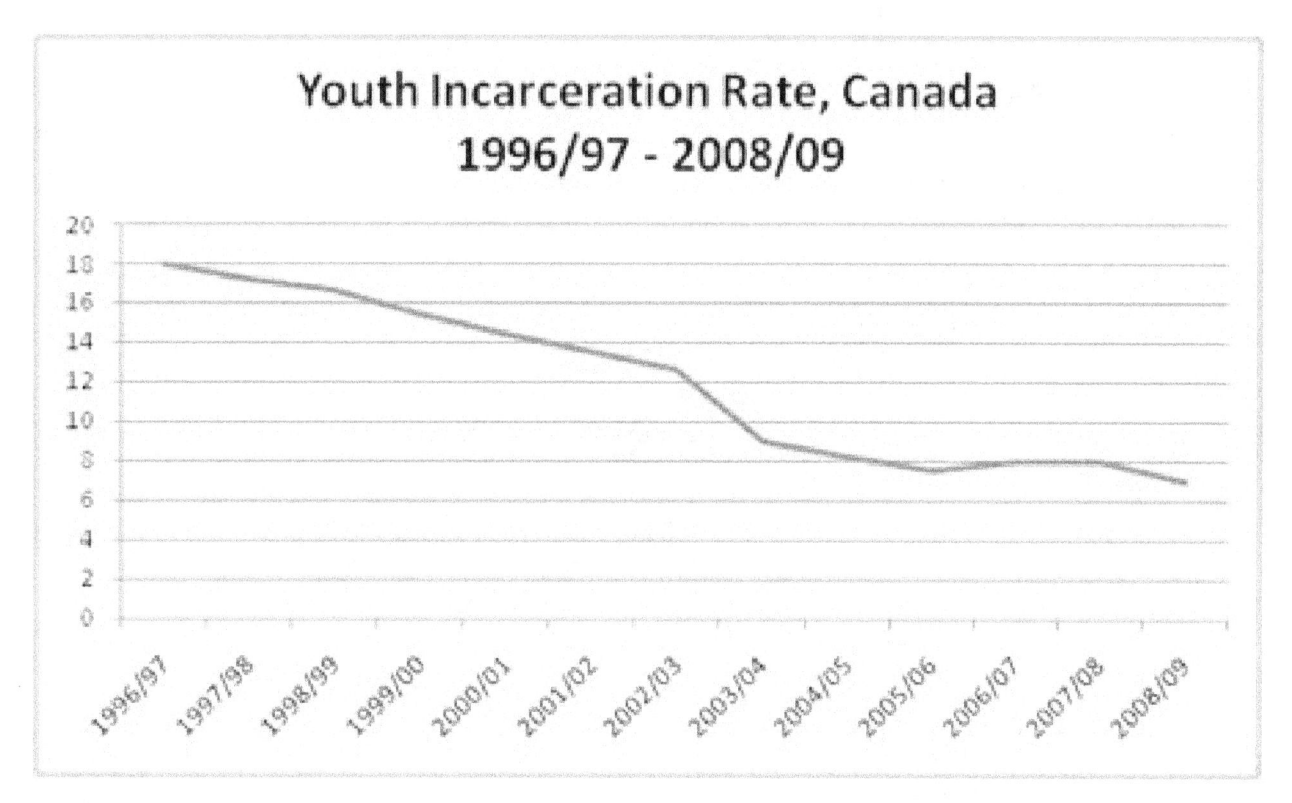

Youth Incarceration Rate, Canada 1996/97 - 2008/09

Source: Canadian Centre for Justice Statistics, Youth Custody and Community Services Survey

Each principal is followed by a list of sub principles, such as rehabilitation, reparations, meaningful consequences, enhanced procedural rights, timely intervention, and notice to victims and parents.

Reparations can include payments or services provided to make up for a victims loss or injury.

The YCJA gives more discretion to the judges by granting them the jurisdiction to impose adult sentences on young persons rather than transferring them to adult court.

Another significant difference from the previous system is a shift in emphasis toward the recognition of victim's rights. Key provisions include:

- The principles of the YCJA specifically recognize the concerns of victims. Victims are to be given information about the proceedings and an opportunity to participate and be heard. They are to be treated with courtesy, compassion and respect for their dignity and privacy.
- Victims have a right of access to youth court records.
- Victims' participation in community-based approaches to responding to offences is encouraged.
- If a young person is dealt with by an extrajudicial sanction, the victim of the offence is entitled to be informed as to how the offence was dealt with.

Many judges are leaning towards diversion programs or extrajudicial measures for youth within the court system. These can include:

Withdrawal of the charge

- Crown attorneys may determine that withdrawal of the charge is appropriate despite the presence of sufficient evidence to proceed with prosecution

Referral to a community agency

- This venue may be appropriate in cases where it is clear that the youth requires assistance with a problem that may have contributed to the offense

Crown caution

- This includes a formal warning from the prosecutor, that although there is enough evidence to proceed with the charge, they have decided not to

Extrajudicial sanctions

- These are the most serious response within the range of extra judicial measures
- These sanction require that the young person accept responsibly for the act that forms the basis of the offence and to comply with terms and conditions of the sanction
- Failure to do so can result in the prosecution of the offence

Depending where you focus your career as a CYC professional, you will likely, at one point and time, have an encounter with a youth who has offended. At this point, the focus, with regards to youth justice, as well as your interactions with the youth, should be towards reducing or eliminating the possibility of that youth reoffending. To that end, the Ministry has created and provided the following information:

The Ministry of Children and Youth Services has undertaken the transformation of youth justice programs and services in order to create a service continuum that reduces reoffending, contributes to community safety and prevents youth crime through rehabilitative programming, holding youth accountable, and creating opportunities for youth at risk.

Reintegration planning and services are intended to address the social, behavioural and environmental needs of youth in conflict with the law. Reintegration planning is a key component of case management planning that helps provide support to youth as they move through, and out of, the justice system. Reintegration services aim to reduce the risk of reoffending, as well as to support successful integration into school, work, home and the community.

The reintegration pathway

Reintegration planning is not a one point in time event, but a continuous process that differs, depending on each youth's circumstances. Reintegration may involve a number of pathways and transition points into, through and eventually, out of the youth justice system. The different reintegration pathways through the youth justice system is as follows (Ontario Ministry of Childrren, Community and Social Services):

Community Sentence (Probation)

Approximately 93%* of youth involved in the youth justice system are serving a community sentence. Probation Officers have responsibility for all aspects of case management for the youth justice mandate. They conduct a Risk Need Assessment to identify strengths and criminogenic needs that are used to establish case management goals. Probation Officers work collaboratively with government funded organizations to share information and provide leadership for collaboration to meet the reintegration goals identified in the case management plan.

Probation, Youth and Family, Community Service Providers: Working in collaboration and sharing information to provide coordinated services to youth

Detention

Youth remanded into detention are awaiting court proceedings. The Detention Initiative was implemented in the fall of 2012, as part of Ontario's Youth Action Plan so that youth on detention are assigned a Probation Officer as a support person for up to 30 days following release. Youth involvement with the Probation officer is voluntary. Reintegration planning is focused on identifying and addressing the basic and immediate needs of youth

Probation, Youth and Family, Community Service Providers: Collaboration, communication, information sharing, coordination

Detention to Community Sentence (Probation)

A youth may receive a community sentence after a period in detention

Probation, Youth and Family, Community Service Providers: Collaboration communication, information sharing, coordination

Detention to Custodial Sentence to Community Supervision (Probation)

Approximately 7%* of youth in the youth justice system are serving a custodial sentence. The Probation Officer provides leadership to the case management team involving facility staff. Transition planning to the community builds on the goals identified in the facility case management reintegration plan.

Under the YCJA, all youth that receive a custodial sentence are required to serve a portion of their sentence in the community. Once a youth is released from custody, the Probation officer continues to provide leadership to the case management team members.

Probation, Youth and Family, Facility Staff, Community Service Providers: Collaboration communication, information sharing, coordination

Reintegration services aim to support successful integration into: school, work, home, and the community, as well as reduce the risk of reoffending.

Source: http://www.children.gov.on.ca

In 2014, the YCJA undertook an initiative to determine the four key outcomes for youth in conflict with the law. The Ministry set new system-wide goals that build on existing efforts to reduce re-offending. Each key outcome has related indicators that define how progress is tracked to allow the Ministry to make evidence-based decision to improve their services across the province.

Four Measurable Outcomes for Youth in Conflict with the Law

1. Outcome - Improved Functioning and Positive Social Behaviours

Indicators

- Increased recognition of impact of behaviours
- Improved social functioning and positive social behaviours
- Decreased risk behaviours

2. Outcome - Increased Skills and Abilities

Indicators

- Increased problem solving ability
- Increased skills and training
- Increased life-skills

3. Outcome - Increased Youth Engagement with Supports

Indicators

- Improved transitions (e.g. with other supports such as mental health)
- Increased youth engagement with community and family supports
- Increased youth engagement with structured supports

4. Outcome - Decreased Re-Offending

Indicators

- Decreased recidivism
- Decreased frequency of offences
- Decreased severity of offences

Source: http://www.children.gov.on.ca

As a CYC you will undoubtedly encounter times when you will need to have an understanding and awareness of both the CYFSA and the YCJA. Always ensure, to the best of your ability, that the child or youth you are working with is adequately represented and that they have an understanding of the process they are involved in.

You will be in a position where you will have to support the youth in your care and withhold judgement, which can often be difficult, especially if you have a moral difference with the behaviours of the youth. However, as a professional, you will rely on your skills and expertise to navigate the system with your client.

Chapter 4 – Let's Reflect

Provide an example of a situation where a diversion program would be recommended for a youth as opposed to pressing charges. Include the expectation you feel should be included in the diversion program.

Chapter 4 - Worksheet

1. What is the main purpose of the CYFSA?

2. What is the age range that the CYFSA applies to?

3. List the 5 forms of maltreatment addressed I the CYFSA?

4. What needs to take place within 30 days once a child is admitted into care?

5. Who has a duty to report?

6. When did the YCJA take over from the YOA?

7. Under the YCJA what type of offenders receives custody sentences?

8. What can reparations include?

9. What shift in emphasis signifies the difference between the previous system and the current system?

10. What are the 4 areas of diversion/extrajudicial measures that the court may use to avoid charges?

Chapter 4 – Checklist

CYFSA:

- ☐ I have read and understood the relevant sections of the CYFSA
- ☐ I have attended a Plan of Care
- ☐ I have reviewed or observed the reviewing of the Rights of the Child
- ☐ I have provided appropriate documentation, that may potentially be used in court, to the jurisdictional agency
- ☐ I am aware of the process of filing a missing person's report in relation to AWOL youth and runaways

YCJA:

- ☐ I have read and understood the relevant sections of the YCJA
- ☐ I have attended youth court with a worker
- ☐ I have attended youth court with a youth
- ☐ I am familiar with extrajudicial measures
- ☐ I understand the role of the probation officer as a member of the multidisciplinary team for the youth

References and Resources

Canadian Centre for Justice Statistics, Youth Custody and Community Services Survey

Canadian Centre for Justice Statistics, Youth Court Survey

Jaime Wegner-Lohin, Alicia Kyte & Nico Trocmé. (2014). Ontario's Child Welfare System. Retrieved from http://cwrp.ca/sites/default/files/publications/en/ON_infosheet_final_0.pdf

Ministry of Children, Community and Social Services. Retrieved from http://www.children.gov.on.ca/

New Learner. (2021). Major differences between the Youth Criminal Justice Act and the Young Offenders Act. Retrieved from http://www.newlearner.com/courses/hts/cln4u/blwho90.htm

Sinha, V., Trocmé, N., Fallon, B., MacLaurin, B., Fast, E., Thomas Prokop, S., Richard, K. (2011). *Kiskisik Awasisak: Remember the Children. Understanding the Overrepresentation of First Nations Children in the Child Welfare System*. Ontario: Assembly of First Nations.

Chapter 5: What Does a CYC Do and Where Do They Do It?

Real Life Story

After I graduated from the 3-year Child and Youth Care program, I began searching for a job. Through my college field placements, I was fortunate enough to work in two school settings and one residential setting. However, by the time I graduated I still had not thought about where my ideal employment setting would be. I wasn't very picky at this point so I handed out resumes to several group homes, one of which was affiliated with the local child protection agency in my jurisdiction. A few weeks after I submitted my resumes I received a phone call from one of the agencies asking me if I would be interested in meeting with them for an interview. They were looking to fill their roster with full time and part time staff. It was a residential program that was just getting started so if I was a successful candidate I would be partially responsible for getting the program off the ground.

The day came for my interview and I attended the group home and waited patiently for the supervisor of the program to arrive. After what seemed like eternity my future supervisor finally showed up. She was very pleasant but she also presented as a 'no nonsense' type of person. I got through the interview and felt quite confident once it was over. I do not recall how long it took for me to hear back from the agency, but when they offered me the job I was elated. This was my first job in the field and I was very proud of myself. What made this even more exciting was the fact that several people that I graduated college with were also hired to work at the group home.

My employment at the group home set the tone for what was yet to come. The experience that I attained from working in a residential setting proved to be invaluable and I will forever appreciate the opportunity that I was given as a new graduate.

Introduction

You have chosen a career in Child and Youth Care. Over the next few years you will be participating in an education program to learn the skills required to obtain a job in the field.

The transition from student to practitioner can be an anxiety producing experience. Evidence has shown that levels of involvement and types of concerns experienced by Child and Youth Care Workers change noticeably during the first three years of employment (Sutton, 1977).

1. Initially the new employee is preoccupied with mastering standard operating procedures
2. Then they tended to compare their work attitudes and philosophies to those co-workers and supervisors
3. Lastly the major focus was their appropriateness for and commitment to the child care role

Sheahan et al. (1987) identified 3 developmental stages that CYC practitioners move through:

1. Finding work
    - Upon graduation, you will begin your job search, utilizing your education as well as the skills used during your placement to secure a job within an environment where you feel most comfortable.
    - You may also change the milieu that you initially considered appropriate for you in favour of an environment where there are more positions available

2. Readiness to Practice
    - As a new graduate and a newly employed CYC practitioner you may question your preparedness to practice, you will notice that the prior focus on learning has changed to one of accountability for the specific client interventions
    - The responsibility of intervening in another human's life can be overwhelming and beginning workers may see their approach as one of trial and error
    - New workers often believe they should know what to do in every situation, however, learning to take positive view of mistakes by accepting and learning from them is a necessary part of adapting to work in Child and Youth Care.

3. Defining the child care role
    - Professional Child and Youth Care has expanded rapidly over the last three decades moving from an almost exclusively institutional base to include a broad range of programs and services (Denholm, Ferguson & Pence, 1987)
    - Lack of role clarity can make it difficult for novice workers to present clear statements about who they are and what they do, CYC's may move into a setting where other professionals are unsure of the role and mandate of the profession and thus are unsure of the contribution that a CYC can bring to a team or agency
    - Unlike other professions, the child care role has flexibility and provides Child and Youth Care Worker with the freedom to adapt their service to meet the "real" needs of the children and families with whom they work.

The following is a list of suggestions which may assist students about to undergo this transition (CYCNet, 2002):

1. Join a Child Care Association. Many CYC practitioners work alone or one on one with clients and will need support, resources and a professional community.
2. Start your networking and a job search while you are still a student. Build your support system and contact list.
3. Be realistic in your expectations of yourself. When you graduate, you will still have a lot to learn. Commit to lifelong learning.

4. Join mailing lists for training seminars, workshops, conferences, and retreats.
5. Frequently touch base with your co workers and supervisors to obtain feedback and skill development.
6. Ensure that you practice self care by developing interests and friendships outside of the field. This work can be exhausting, emotional and depleting, you need to find balance and a way to re charge.
7. Find a support system comprised of people who will understand your work and with whom you can share the highs and lows, who will listen and share ideas.

Every job is classified by a NOC code (National Occupational Classification code) which is basically a tool that is used to classify occupations according to skill level and skill type. Every occupation is identified by a four-number code, called the NOC code. Each number represents a different trait, which describes the type of industry, and the education and skills required.

4212 - Social and Community Service Workers

Social and community service workers administer and implement a variety of social assistance programs and community services, and assist clients to deal with personal and social problems. They are employed by social service and government agencies, mental health agencies, group homes, shelters, substance abuse centres, school boards, correctional facilities and other establishments.

Illustrative example(s)

- Aboriginal Outreach Worker
- Addictions Worker
- **Child and Youth Worker**
- Community Development Worker
- Community Service Worker
- Crisis Intervention Worker
- Developmental Service Worker
- Drop-In Centre Worker
- Family Service Worker
- Group Home Worker
- Income Maintenance Officer - Social Services
- Life Skills Instructor
- Mental Health Worker
- Rehabilitation Worker - Social Services
- Social Services Worker
- Veteran Services Officer
- Welfare and Compensation Officer
- Women's Shelter Supervisor
- Youth Worker

Exclusion(s)

- Activities leaders - seniors (See 5254 Program leaders and instructors in recreation, sport and fitness)
- Educational counsellors (4033)
- Family, marriage and other related counsellors (4153)
- Instructors of persons with disabilities (4215)
- Managers in social, community and correctional services (0423)
- Social workers (4152)

Main duties

- Social and community service workers perform some or all of the following duties:
- Review client background information, interview clients to obtain case history and prepare intake reports
- Assess clients' relevant skill strengths and needs
- Assist clients to sort out options and develop plans of action while providing necessary support and assistance
- Assess and investigate eligibility for social benefits
- Refer clients to other social services or assist clients in locating and utilizing community resources including legal, medical and financial assistance, housing, employment, transportation, day care and other services
- Counsel clients living in group homes and half-way houses, supervise their activities and assist in pre-release and release planning
- Participate in the selection and admission of clients to appropriate programs
- Implement life skills workshops, substance abuse treatment programs, behaviour management programs, youth services programs and other community and social service programs under the supervision of social services or health care professionals
- Meet with clients to assess their progress, give support and discuss any difficulties or problems
- Assist in evaluating the effectiveness of treatment programs by tracking clients' behavioural changes and responses to interventions
- Advise and aid recipients of social assistance and pensions
- Provide crisis intervention and emergency shelter services
- Implement and organize the delivery of specific services within the community
- Maintain contact with other social service agencies and health care providers involved with clients to provide information and obtain feedback on clients' overall progress
- Co-ordinate the volunteer activities of human service agencies, health care facilities and arts and sports organizations
- May maintain program statistics for purposes of evaluation and research
- May supervise social service support workers and volunteers.

Employment requirements

- Completion of a college or university program in Social Work, Child and Youth Care, Psychology or other social science or health-related discipline is usually required.

- Previous work experience in a social service environment as a volunteer or in a support capacity may replace formal education requirements for some occupations in this unit group.
- Social service workers may be required to be a member of a provincial regulatory body in some provinces.

Additional information

- Progression to professional occupations in social services, such as family and marriage counsellors, social workers, and probation and parole officers, is possible with additional training and experience.

    Source: Statistics Canada, National Occupational Classification (NOC) 2011

There are various environments where Child and Youth Care Practitioners are required and through your education and placement experiences you will learn where your skills and preferences are best suited.

Child and Youth Care Workers often work as part of a team of social workers, psychologists, recreation therapists, foster care workers, teachers and other professionals. They help integrate the efforts of all these specialized professionals with children, youth and families who may be experiencing emotional or behavioural challenges. Due to their on-going close involvement with children, youth and families, Child and Youth Care Workers are in an ideal position to help these individuals to be advocates for themselves and to take responsibility for their actions.

Child and Youth Care Workers must be familiar with the developmental, educational, emotional, social and recreational needs of young people as well as the family system. Employers generally prefer to hire applicants who have related post-secondary education, preferably a diploma or degree in Child and Youth Care or a related social science or human services degree. Previous work experience with young people is a definite asset. In some settings, knowledge of native culture and language may be required.

The employment outlook in this occupation will be influenced by a wide variety of factors including (Health Warriors nework):

- trends and events affecting overall employment (especially in the industries listed above)
- employment turnover (work opportunities generated by people leaving existing positions)
- occupational growth (work opportunities resulting from the creation of new positions that never existed before)
- employment turnover is expected to increase as members of the baby boom generation retire over the next ten years.

The employment outlook will be fair for Social and community service workers (NOC 4212; which includes CYC Practitioners)) in the Toronto region for the 2019-2021 period.

The following factors contributed to this outlook:

- employment growth will lead to several new positions.
- not many positions will become available due to retirements.
- there are a small number of unemployed workers with recent experience in this occupation.

Here are some key facts about Social and community service workers in the Toronto region (Jobback Canada):

- approximately 15,310 people work in this occupation.
- social and community service workers mainly work in the following sectors:
- nursing and residential care facilities and social assistance (NAICS 623-624): 49%
- ambulatory health care services and hospitals (NAICS 621-622): 11%
- other services (except public administration) (NAICS 81): 10%
- educational services (NAICS 61): 10%
- local, municipal, regional, aboriginal and other public administration (NAICS 913-919): 8%

School-Based Setting

My first college field placement was in a school setting. I completed two school field placements. The first one was more of an observational placement. I did not have many responsibilities and my main objective was to observe the students and be an extra support person for the classroom teacher. The expectations for the second year field placement were much different. By year two I was expected to take initiative and apply what I learned in the classrooms. The responsibilities of a Child and Youth Care Practitioner in a classroom can vary. You might be responsible for supporting a single student on a one-on-one basis. This support might be academic, behavioral or both. You might be asked to support whoever requires support in your class or you might be asked to provide support to students throughout the school.

From my experience working in school based settings, the following are some of the responsibilities that a Child and Youth Practitioner might have:

- to ensure that the school setting is a safe and predictable environment for the students
- maintain clear communication with students, their families and community professionals
- report and document all serious occurrences and incidents that involve the safety and security of students and staff
- ensure that the treatment component is being taught and utilized within the day-to-day academic environment
- clearly document recordings and treatment plans for all students in your care
- administer medication and ensure that all documentation is clear and concise
- maintain up to date training

Hospital Setting

Throughout my career as a Child and Youth Practitioner I have worked in 3 three hospitals and one treatment center. I worked in the mental health unit in those hospitals. My employment at the treatment center focused on immediate and short-term mental health interventions for children and adolescents. Each unit provided stabilization, assessment and intensive treatment for children and adolescents who presented with urgent and emotional difficulties. Within these therapeutic milieus a Child and Youth Practitioner may work with nurses, psychiatrists, dieticians, educational specialists and psychologists.

The roles of a Child and Youth Practitioner working in a hospital or treatment center include:

- conducts thorough safety assessments of clients who present themselves to the hospital/treatment center
- to ensure that the environment is safe and predictable for clients, caregivers and staff

- maintain clear communication with clients, their families and community professionals
- report and document all serious occurrences and incidents that involve the safety and security of clients and staff
- ensure that the treatment component is being taught and utilized within the day to day academic environment
- provide one to one support to clients as needed
- assist the therapeutic team in the stabilization of clients on the unit
- maintain up to date training

Residential/Group Home Setting

Working in a group home or residential setting definitely tests all of your skills as a Child and Youth Care Practitioner. You are there for the clients when they wake up in the morning and you are there when they go to sleep at night. The responsibilities of a CYC in a residential setting are long and sometimes challenging due in part to the amount of time that you will spend with the residents. As a CYC you will interact with the residents during day shifts, evening shifts and overnight shifts. You will notice differences in their behavior before, during and after visits with their families and caregivers. You will observe changes in their moods during weekdays compared to how they respond to you on weekends.

It is very important to maintain appropriate professional boundaries in this setting because the youth are highly likely to perceive you as a family member. Setting firm boundaries and clear expectations with clients early on in the relationship is highly recommended.

The roles of a Child and Youth Practitioner working in a group home or residential setting include:

- conduct thorough admission and discharge assessments of clients. This may include admission medicals, discharge medicals, clothing and belonging inventory and review of rights and responsibilities
- to ensure that the environment is safe and predictable for clients, caregivers and staff
- maintain clear communication with clients, their families and community professionals
- report and document all serious occurrences and incidents that involve the safety and security of clients and staff
- complete missing person reports as deemed necessary
- administer medication to all clients as deemed necessary
- complete medication checks as deemed necessary
- provide one to one support to clients as needed
- maintain mandatory training
- coordinate and schedule access visits with family members and caregivers as deemed necessary
- complete daily logs and maintain professional written and verbal communication internally and externally
- attend plans of care meetings
- maintain up to date training

Child Welfare Setting

Within a child welfare setting there are numerous positions that a Child and Youth Practitioner can acquire. There is a high opportunity for growth and development in the child welfare environment due in part to the maintenance and creation of many valuable and creative positions. Positions include supervised access workers, children services workers, family services workers, family support workers, kinship workers and intake workers.

The roles of a Child and Youth Practitioner working in a child welfare setting include:

- supervising scheduled access visits between children, youth and adolescents and their family members/caregivers as deemed necessary
- complying with plans of care and ONLAC (Ontario looking after children) requirements as deemed necessary by Ministry guidelines
- conducting safety and risk assessments as deemed necessary when conducting child protection investigations
- maintaining regular contact and communication with children, youth, adolescents and their family/caregivers as deemed necessary by Ministry guidelines
- referring children, youth, adolescents and their family/caregivers to programs that are deemed appropriate to their needs
- maintain up to date reports and documentation
- provide family members/caregivers with strategies and techniques that can assist them in managing the behaviors of their child/children
- work closely with internal colleagues and external community partners to meet the best interest of the child/children

Regardless of where you work, or what population of children and youth you work with, you will likely find your career as a Child and Youth Care practitioner a very rewarding one. As with any job related to working with people, your days will always be varied, and you will learn to expect the unexpected. You will soon recognize that each day is not perfect, you will second guess yourself, you will potentially be injured, you will likely end up in tears more than once, you may even threaten to leave the field all together; however when a youth you have been working with finally has a breakthrough or a success, your level of pride will know no bounds.

We wish you the best of luck as you complete your education and pursue your career!

Chapter 5 - Let's Reflect

If you were able to choose the perfect environment for you to work in as a child and youth care practitioner, what would that look like and why did you choose this specific milieu?

Chapter 5 - Let's Reflect

Chapter 5 – Worksheet

1. List 5 of the general duties as described in the NOC code 4212.

2. Using information in this chapter, define and discuss the 3 phases that a CYC practitioner goes through after finding their first job within the field.

3. Name 3 different environments where CYC practitioner can find employment.

4. Explain 2 key differences between residential, school based, child protection & hospital settings.

Chapter 5 Checklist

- ☐ I am familiar with the NOC code for a CYC
- ☐ I am aware of the general job description and duties of a CYC
- ☐ I am knowledgeable of agencies who hire CYC practitioners in my area
- ☐ I am aware of the employment outlook for CYC practitioner s
- ☐ I know the 3 stages a new CYC may go through after finding their first job
- ☐ I understand the potential difficulty/concerns re:
    - ☐ Finding work
    - ☐ Readiness to practice
    - ☐ Defining the CYC role
- ☐ I am familiar with the requirements of a CYC in a school setting
- ☐ I am familiar with the job requirements for a CYC in a hospital setting
- ☐ I am familiar with the job requirements for a CYC in a child protection setting
- ☐ I am familiar with the job requirements for a CYC in a residential setting
- ☐ I know how to become a member of my local Child and Youth Care association
- ☐ I have begun building my professional network
- ☐ I have charted a course for my continued personal and professional development
- ☐ I have registered to receive updates regarding CYC related training seminars, workshops conferences and retreats
- ☐ I have a plan to become proactive in soliciting support and feedback from my supervisors and colleagues
- ☐ I will ensure that I practice self-care and develop interests and friendships outside of the field
- ☐ I have a group of people who support my work and understand my profession

References and Resource

Health Warriors Network. Retrieved from http://healthwarriors.ca/journey/browse/careers/child-youth-care-worker/

Job Bank Canada. Retrieved from https://www.jobbank.gc.ca/marketreport/outlook-occupation/5112/22437

Moscrip, S. and A. Brown. (2002). Child and youth care: The transition from student to practitioner. CYCNet, 41(June). Retrieved from https://www.cyc-net.org/cyc-online/cycol-0602-transitions.html

Sutton, B. (1977). Consideration of career time in child care work experiences. Child Care Quarterly, 6, 121-126.

Statistics Canada, National Occupational Classification (NOC) 2011. Retrieved from https://www23.statcan.gc.ca/imdb/p3VD.pl?Function=getVD&TVD=122372&CVD=122376&CPV=4212&CST=01012011&MLV=4&CLV=4

Chapter 6: What is Abuse and How Does it Impact Children and Adolescents?

Real Life Story

Please note that the names of the individuals involved will be changed to maintain privacy and anonymity. Early in my career I worked as a Children's Services Worker. I was responsible for supporting children, youth and adolescents in a variety of placements such as foster homes, group homes, and treatment facilities. I had 3 children placed in a foster home. Shawn and Jacob were siblings and Harrison was the third child on my caseload in the foster home. Shawn was 3-years-old, Jacob was 11 months old and Harrison was one-year-old. One afternoon while I was supervising an access visit between Jacob, Shawn and their parents, I noticed something peculiar about the appearance of Jacob while his parents were changing his diaper. My youngest son just happened to be the same age as Jacob and they shared the same birthday. In my head I was thinking how much smaller Jacob seemed compared to my son. From the naked eye, Jacob appeared to be approximately 5 to 10 pounds lighter than my son. Furthermore, Jacob's overall appearance looked unusual. My instincts told me that something was wrong. One of our High Risk Infant Nurses happened to walk by the access room so I asked her if she could do a quick assessment of Jacob. While the nurse was gone I explained to the parents that I was concerned with Jacob's weight and I wanted to ensure that nothing was wrong. The nurse returned and placed Jacob on the scale. Jacob was severely underweight, and he did not even register on the Ages and Stages growth chart.

I immediately consulted with my supervisor because all of the children were scheduled to return to the foster home and we needed to figure out why Jacob was underweight. Whenever there are concerns of child abuse, our agency will consult with the Suspected Child Abuse and Neglect team at Sick Children's Hospital. Given the fact that Jacob was so young we could not take any risks and decided to consult with the S.C.A.N team. We contacted the team and consulted with them on the telephone. They asked that we bring all three boys to the hospital for them to be fully assessed. They did not want to take any chances and neither did we.

We transported the children to Sick Kid's Hospital and made our way to the S.C.AN team. Once there, each child was put through a battery of tests that included blood tests and X-rays. The results were far from what my supervisor and I had expected. Shawn had a historical fracture on his shin, Jacob had a skull fracture and Harrison had a fracture on his forearm. Although the team could not ascertain when each injury occurred, they were able to determine that injuries were not present prior to each child coming into care. This meant that these injuries were induced while they were in foster care. Furthermore, the S.C.A.N team also concluded that the injuries appeared to be inflicted by an outside source. The children did not obtain these injuries as a result of regular child play.

> All of the children were removed from the foster home and a joint investigation was launched with the police. The foster parents were charged, and the matter went before the courts. However, the truth never did come out as to how the children sustained these injuries.with the police. The foster parents were charged, and the matter went before the courts. However, the truth never did come out as to how the children sustained these injuries.
>
> This is an example of how physical abuse is not always something that can be observed visually. It is also more difficult to ascertain abuse if the children are at a young age (chronologically or developmentally) and are nonverbal. X-rays and intrusive medical assessments were required for us to figure out that these young children had significant injuries. If not for the fact that Jacob was severely underweight, who knows how long it would have taken for somebody to notice that these children were being abused.

Introduction

An important factor in assessing and supporting children, youth and adolescents as a Child and Youth Practitioner is the ability to recognize and identify the signs and symptoms of child abuse. A lone indicator or a series of indicators is not necessarily a sign that a child is being abused. However, it certainly is crucial that all suspicions be reported to the proper authorities for further investigation. Child abuse suspicions should always be investigated by the Police and/or a Child Protection Agency.

In your role as a Child and Youth Practitioner, it is important to understand and be familiar with the normal stages of development in children and adolescents. Knowledge of child and adolescent development will assist you in determining whether some of the challenges you observe in the children you work with are part of their normal development or if there may be other factors contributing to their behavior.

Child abuse is generally categorized into four major areas: neglect, physical, sexual and emotional maltreatment. Ontario has recently included children exposed to domestic violence as another category of child maltreatment which will be discussed later in this chapter. Although these five areas may be categorized separately, it is quite common for children to be affected by more than one form of abuse simultaneously. Child abuse and neglect can occur as a single isolated incident or it can be an ongoing pattern of many incidents involving one or more types of abuse.

There is no doubt that child-rearing is a difficult and challenging task. There are no policy and procedure manuals for raising a child, however, there are many resources available to assist parents.

Parental capacity is not something that can fit into a box as every family and situation is unique. Each family has its own strengths, weaknesses and areas in which they can improve.

However, concern can arise if the parents do not have the "capacity" to parent due to issues related to addictions, domestic violence, mental health issues and developmental issues.

Regardless of the issue that has impacted a family's capacity to parent, it is almost universal that if parenting capacity is compromised the child will suffer from some form of neglect and emotional abuse.

In this chapter we will address several behavior issues of caregivers that can impact parenting capacity and the neglect that likely follows, and we will discuss the responses of the children to these environments.

Physical Abuse

Physical abuse is the application of force to any part of a child's body, which results or may result in a non-accidental injury. Physical abuse may include but is not limited to shaking, choking, biting, kicking, burning, poisoning or any other harmful or dangerous use of force or restraint. Most child physical abuse is associated with physical punishment or is often confused with disciplinary tactics. Physical abuse can lead to permanent injury or in worse case scenarios, death.

Indicators of Physical Abuse

There may be some indicators that a child is being physically abused. However, not all indicators will be visible with the naked eye. If a child is suffering from internal injuries more intrusive testing may be part of the investigation process such as an MRI, X-ray or a CT scan. These tests are usually arranged in collaboration with the Child Protection agency, Police and medical professionals. Here are several signs that might indicate that a child is being physically abused:

- unexplained or suspicious marks/bruises
- marks or bruises located in uncommon areas of the body, e.g., behind the ears, behind the knees and on the genitals
- the explanation for the injury that is given by the child and/or parent or caregiver is not consistent with the actual injury
- the child reports that he/she is being physically abused
- breaks and/or fractures in the bones of infants and toddlers
- burns and scalds
- injuries to the abdominal area
- human bite marks

Sexual Abuse

Sexual abuse occurs when an adult or youth uses a child for sexual purposes. Sexual abuse includes fondling, intercourse, incest, sodomy, exhibitionism, and exploitation through prostitution or the production of pornographic materials. Sexual abuse can occur inside and outside the family unit.

The definition of abusive sexual activity includes but is not limited to:

- Sexual Intercourse: oral, anal and genital penetration
- Sexual Molestation: fondled breast or genitals, offender made the child exhibit himself/herself, but there was no sexual intercourse
- Sexual Exhibitionism: person has exhibited himself/herself in front of the child – exposure of genitals, masturbation
- Sexual Harassment: child is encouraged, pressured or propositioned to perform sexually -- No sexual physical activity has actually occurred
- Sexual Suggestiveness: sexually provocative comments are made to a child, child is shown pornographic images

- Other Sexual Abuse: exploitation for the purpose of pornography, voyeurism, observation of adult sexual behavior, "grooming" activities

Child Sexual Exploitation

Child sexual exploitation on the Internet takes many forms and there are also interconnections between sexual abuse through prostitution and trafficking that exists on a global level. Child pornography on the web represents a permanent record of a sexual crime being committed. Once those images are distributed over the Internet, they can never be eradicated, and they serve to perpetuate the victimization of the children. The victims will always know that the obscene images are available on the Internet for a future partner, child or colleague to stumble across. In Canada there is a fast growing problem regarding child trafficking, specifically in Ontario. In order to address this dilemma, the Ontario government has invested $307 million on a new anti-human trafficking strategy.

In 2016, a joint research project on child trafficking was conducted between York University, York CAS and the York Region Police Services. The data concluded that a significant number of the child trafficking cases involved females who were Crown Wards who were under the age of 17.

The types of abuse described above are by commission, meaning that someone "committed" the abuse. Neglect is often created by omission, meaning that something required was "omitted from the care of the child. Any form of abuse is unacceptable regardless if it was abuse by commission or omission.

Indicators of Sexual abuse

- The child may have an unusual fascination with the genital area
- The child may display poor boundaries with people
- The child may engage in inappropriate sexual play
- The child may flinch when approached by people
- The child may display inappropriate knowledge of sexual terminology or slang

Please note that the above indicators do not necessarily mean that a child/youth is being sexually abused. However, if one or more of the indicators is present in a child, further assessment should be initiated.

Neglect

Neglect is the chronic inattention to the necessities in life such as:

- clothing
- shelter
- food
- education
- good hygiene
- supervision
- medical and dental care
- adequate rest
- safe environment
- exercise
- fresh air

Real Life Story

Rebecca was a mother of two children named Felix and Felicia. Felix was 15-years-old and Felicia was 7-years-old. Rebecca ran a daycare out of her home and took care of 3 children. Janelle was 9-years-old, Terrence was 6-years-old and Levi was 2-years-old.

After being picked up by her mother, on the ride home Janelle told Maria that she no longer wanted to be babysat by Rebecca. Janelle insisted that she could stay home after school by herself until her mother returned from work. Maria told Janelle that she would have to wait a few more years until she was able to be left alone. Janelle started to cry and appeared to be extremely upset. Maria asked Janelle why she was so upset and adamant about wanting to stop going to Rebecca's house after school. Janelle told her mother that Rebecca's son Felix made her feel uncomfortable. Maria asked Janelle to explain what she meant and assured Janelle that she would not be in any trouble. Janelle hesitated and then stated that Felix asked her to suck his penis. Maria was shocked but managed to maintain calmness while she encouraged Janelle to provide more details. Once Janelle was finished with her disclosure, Maria contacted the police who in turn contacted the local Child Protection Agency.

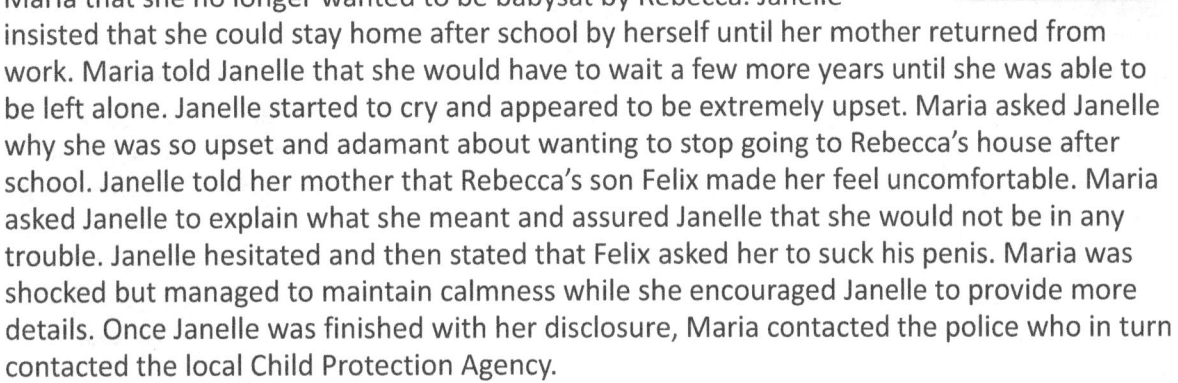

Rebecca was notified of the allegations and her home daycare was immediately put on hold during the investigation. The police and the Child Protection Agency conducted a joint investigation which included but was not limited to interviews of the alleged victim, her mother, the other daycare children and the babysitter and her children. Based on the information that was obtained from the numerous interviews the police eventually charged Felix with one count of sexual interference and one count of sexual assault.

Indicators of Neglect

Here are some physical indicators of neglect in children, youth and adolescents:

- A child that is often left unsupervised for unacceptable amounts of time (See Supervision Guidelines). This depends on the age and maturity level of the child.
- The child is not appropriately dressed based on the weather conditions (young child is not provided with mittens during cold weather).
- The child consistently comes to school without a lunch and/or snack.
- The child has very poor oral and physical hygiene.
- The child might appear to be malnourished.
- The child may have poor school attendance
- The child may be overly compliant with adults.
- The child's caregivers might consistently miss the child's scheduled medical appointments.

Real Life Story

Bonnie was diagnosed with anxiety when she was 14-years-old. Bonnie didn't have any siblings but she had a very supportive and nurturing relationship with her parents. Bonnie's parents tried to get help for her but she was against any form of treatment because she felt that all teenagers went through this phase so in her mind she would eventually, "snap out of it". As time went on Bonnie's mental health worsened and she began to abuse illicit substances on a regular basis. The use of drugs combined with Bonnie's frail mental health only exacerbated an already serious condition. Miraculously, Bonnie graduated high school but chose to leave home shortly afterwards because she felt that her parents were putting too many restrictions on her freedom. Bonnie became transient and moved from shelter to shelter over a 2-year span. When Bonnie turned 19-years-old she became pregnant with a son named Tyler and ended up living in subsidized housing. Although Bonnie did receive pre-natal care while pregnant, once Tyler was born she ceased to communicate or accept help from any of her support systems. Many months passed before Bonnie finally allowed her Healthy Babies worker to conduct a home visit in order to check on the wellbeing of Tyler. When the worker attended the home she could hear Tyler crying at the top of his lungs as if he was in distress. The worker knocked on the door and Bonnie answered. When the worker entered the home she could smell the distinct aroma of marijuana and alcohol. The worker asked Bonnie if she was under the influence of an illegal substance and Bonnie denied that she was high. The worker observed Tyler as he was sitting in his car seat. She picked Tyler up and immediately suspected that he was underweight. She then laid Tyler onto the floor and assessed his muscle tone, strength and motor skills. Tyler's head was also very flat which indicated that he spent a lot of time on his back unattended. Following the assessment, the worker advised Bonnie that she had no other choice than to contact child protection services due to the serious concerns related to Tyler's health and well-being. Bonnie stated that she did not care if Tyler was removed from her care and then proceeded to pack some of his belongings. Child protection services arrived shortly afterwards and Tyler was apprehended from Bonnie's care and then taken to a foster home.

Emotional Abuse

Emotional abuse can be described as the repetitive emotional response to the child's expression of emotions. Emotional abuse might be one of the most difficult forms of abuse to recognize or verify. In contrast to physical or sexual abuse, emotional abuse does not always present itself with physical indicators. Emotional abuse is usually present in all the forms of abuse. The indicators of emotional abuse are usually behavioral.

Indicators of Emotional Abuse

Emotional abuse can be difficult to identify in a child or youth. Unlike some forms of physical abuse, there are often no visuals signs that can assist a person in determining whether or not a child is being emotionally abused. When it is confirmed that a child or youth is being emotionally abused, you will often find that there may be several other forms of abuse present as well, for example:

- lags in developmental milestones
- depression, anxiety
- overly compliant behavior
- attention seeking behavior
- obsessed with cleanliness

Exposure to Family Violence

A child or youth can experience familial or domestic violence when he/she is exposed to verbal, physical or emotional abuse between members of the family. Although children being exposed to domestic violence has always been concerning, very thorough reviews of cases were conducted, and the results showed that prolonged exposure to domestic violence can negatively impact the overall wellbeing and development of a child/youth. Further studies have shown that children may often become physically injured as a result of simply being present during a domestic conflict. Children and youth may attempt to protect their caregiver and as a result might be unintentionally struck during the physical conflict.

Real Life Story

In Child Protection, when investigations involve Community Caregivers, these cases are assigned to specialized workers called Serious Occurrence Workers to investigate. A Community Caregiver is a person who is responsible for the well-being of a child, youth or adolescent. Community Caregivers can include teachers, coaches, counselors, foster parents and group home staff. Any person or persons who are in charge of looking after children, youth or adolescents are considered to be Community Caregivers.

We often receive referrals from parents of children who are involved in high level sports such as Representative Hockey, Basketball and Baseball. This level of sport is very demanding and sometimes the coaches of Representative sports leagues place a lot of stress and anxiety on the players.

I have conducted several investigations involving coaches who have been accused of being verbally abusive towards players. Parents, children and witnesses have reported that coaches have been overheard calling players derogatory names in front of their peers. Further accusations of belittling, yelling and public humiliation have also been reported.

Victims of this type of abuse will often report feeling extremely anxious and embarrassed because of the actions of a coach. Parents are not always immediately aware of what is going on because they are not always permitted to be present during all practices. Therefore, this type of behavior may go on for long periods of time before the abuse is reported. Other players may not report their observations for fear of being benched or not chosen for the team.

Physical indicators of a child exposed to Family Violence

- sleep disruption
- aggressive behavior (physical or verbal)
- bullying (physical or verbal)
- bedwetting or bed soiling
- highly anxious behavior
- frequent absences from school
- somatic complaints (headaches or stomach aches)
- regression (child can no longer carry out tasks that he/she had previously mastered)
- withdrawal (child is no longer interested in activities that he/she was previously interested in)

Real Life Story

Caleb was an 11-year-old boy in grade 6. Caleb didn't have any friends, acted out in class and had the tendency to be physically and verbally aggressive towards his teachers and support staff. Multiple meetings with Caleb's parents were arranged in the past to discuss Caleb's behavior but only Caleb's mother would attend. When asked about the whereabouts of Caleb's father, Caleb's mother would usually advise the staff team that he was either working or busy with other commitments. One day Caleb's teacher advised the class that it was time to get ready for French. Caleb and his peers had been working on an art project, one of a few subjects that Caleb enjoys. Caleb's peers followed the teacher's instructions and began to put away and clean up their art supplies. However, focused and determined to continue working on his artwork, Caleb ignored the request made by his teacher and continued to work on his art. Caleb's teacher politely and gently asked Caleb to get ready for French but he ignored her and stated that he wasn't done yet. Caleb's peer's had already put away their materials and were patiently waiting for Caleb to follow suit. One of Caleb's peers shouted, "Here we go again." Upon hearing this, Caleb got up from his desk, walked over to the student and slapped him across the face. Caleb's teacher paged the office and requested support from the principal. The two support staff in the classroom began to evacuate the other students out of the classroom and into the hallway. By the time the principal made it to the classroom, all of the students except for Caleb were standing in the hallway. The principal directed Caleb to accompany him to his office where he would have to spend the remainder of the day.

While walking to the principal's office, Caleb began to cry. The principal asked Caleb what was wrong and Caleb responded by telling the principal that once his father found out about what happened, he'd be upset. Caleb further stated that his father had recently been aggressive towards him and his mother and this incident would make him even more upset. The principal put his hand on Caleb's shoulder and then walked him the remainder of the way to his office. Once in the office, the principal called the local child protection agency.

Canadian Statistics

Statistics from 2018 indicated that female victims accounted for 57% of the 60,651 reported cases of child abuse that involved children and youth victims aged 17 and younger.

Overall 32% of the abusers were acquaintances, 31% were family members, and 17% were abused by an unknown assailant.

As shown in Figure 6.1, child abuses cases that involved family members as perpetrators increased by 1% between 2009 and 2018, while non-family violence decreased by 31%.

Figure 6.1 – Child and Youth Victims of Police-reported Family and Non-family Violence, by Sex and Year, 2009 to 2018

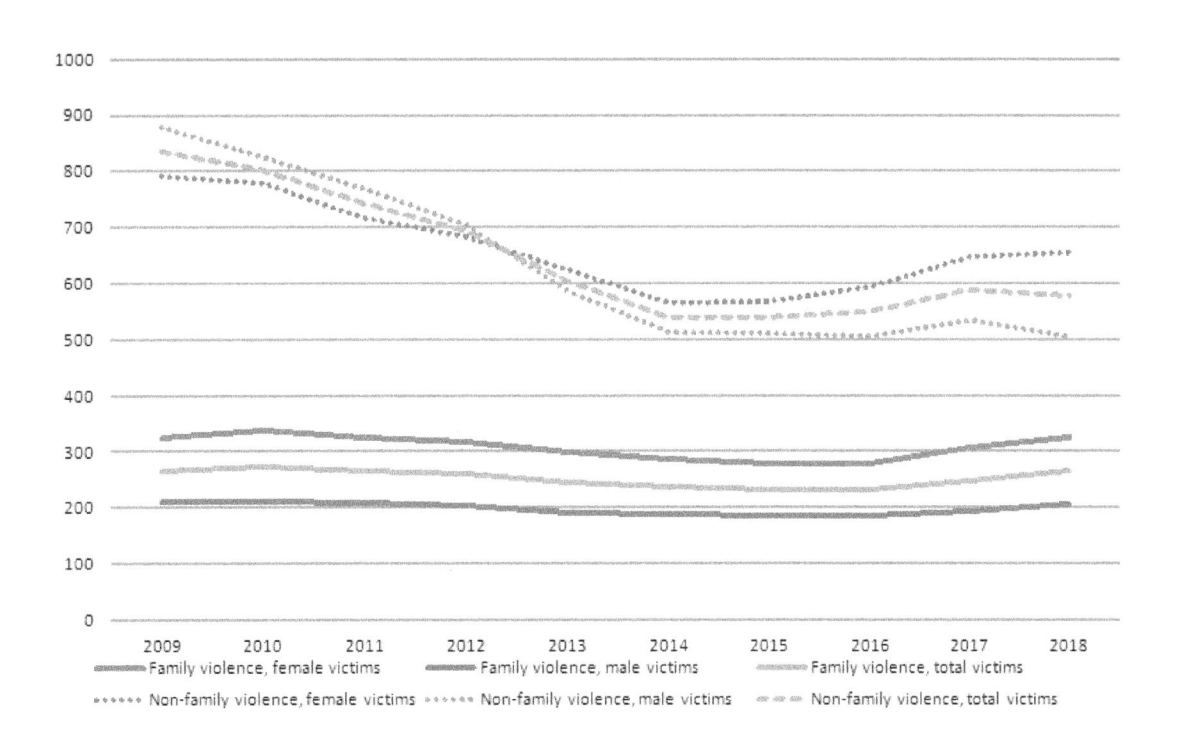

Source: Statistics Canada, Canadian Centre for Justice Statistics, Incident-based Uniform Crime Reporting Survey, Trend Database

The number of family violence incidents that were reported to the police which involved a parent as the accused perpetrator was 19% by 2018 and children under the age of 5 accounted for approximately 53% of this total. Adolescents between the ages of 15 and 17-years-old reported 8% of family violence committed by a parent. The majority of child/youth victims were victimized at a residence location.

In 2018 family-related sexual offences perpetrated against children and youth was 266 per 100,000. This number increased from 159 per 100,000 when the child and youth victims were 5-years-old and younger. When the victims were between the ages of 15 to 17-years-old the number increased to 379 per 100,000.

Physical assaults continued to be a frequently disclosed form of family violence at 75%. One in six incidents involved a weapon of which one in four experienced some minor physical injury. Injury was more common for male victims than for females.

Chapter 6 – Let's Reflect

When reflecting on the different types of child abuse do you feel that in every circumstance the child will always suffer from emotional abuse? If so, explain and support your answer.

Chapter 6 - Worksheet

- Indicate some of the signs of physical abuse.

- Indicate some of the signs of sexual abuse.

- Indicate some of the signs of neglect.

- Indicate some of the signs of emotional abuse.

- Indicate some indicators of a child who is exposed to domestic violence.

- If you gain knowledge of a child who is being abused, what steps should you take to ensure the safety of the child?

- What is the most common type of family violence?

Chapter 6 – Checklist

- ☐ I can confidently list the signs of physical abuse
- ☐ I can confidently list the signs of sexual abuse
- ☐ I can confidently list the signs of neglect
- ☐ I can confidently list the signs of emotional abuse
- ☐ I can confidently list the signs of a child who is exposed to domestic violence
- ☐ I am familiar with the Canadian statistics regarding child abuse and its impact on families and children

References and Resources

Statistics Canada, Canadian Centre for Justice Statistics, Incident-based Uniform Crime Reporting Survey, Trend Database

Chapter 7: What is a Therapeutic Relationship and How Do I Create Professional Boundaries?

> ### Real Life Story
>
> A recently graduated CYC had built a strong rapport and therapeutic relationship with a youth whom she saw on a weekly basis. They had developed a high level of trust and the strategies the CYC suggested and supported had resulted in positive outcomes for the youth.
>
> The CYC was the first individual who had consistently remained in the youth's life, despite his issues and behaviors.
>
> The youth frequently would invite the CYC out into the community on social occasions; however the care worker consistently refused. The youth would tell his worker that they were so close in age that they would probably have been friends outside of the therapeutic relationships had they met under different circumstances.
>
> The CYC had completed her work with the youth and he was discharged from her care.
>
> Approximately 2 months later the CYC was out at a party and the youth happened to be at the same event.
>
> The CYC and the youth both remained at the party where drinking was involved. The next day, on social media, a picture of the 2 of them together, linking arms and drinking beer surfaced.
>
> The CYC was called into her manager's office and was fired on the spot.

Therapeutic Relationship

It is often difficult to maintain therapeutic boundaries when working within the helping professions; however, it is paramount for the client's wellbeing and your career to ensure that boundaries and ethics are implemented.

Child and Youth Care Practitioners work with children and youth as an holistic individual, in order to support their social interactions and healthy development. They facilitate this by participating in and using their natural environments on a day to day basis, and their life experiences, while developing a therapeutic relationship with their clients (Anglin, 2001).

The practice of Child and Youth Care begins with the development of a therapeutic relationship within any environment. It is possible that this might be the first intimate connection that a youth or child may have had with another person. This places the CYC Worker in a special role of being responsible for providing a safe, nurturing setting that allows the child/youth to explore their feelings openly.

In order to do this, the CYC Practitioner has to maintain appropriate boundaries that fit within a therapeutic, professional relationship, which is different from a personal relationship.

In a professional relationship (Davidson, 2009):

- the practitioners' authority, knowledge, influence, and access to privileged information places the practitioner in a postion of authority
- the focus is on the client's needs
- the relationship is based on trust
- the relationship inevitably comes to an end
- the relationship may be legally sanctioned
- the relationship is shaped by the practitioner's formal knowledge, skills and training
- the practitioner is paid to provide care
- the goal is to promote positive change
- the practitioner is required to remain objective
- the practitioner has to establish and maintain professional boundaries

Carl Rogers (1951) emphasizes three qualities that a Child and Youth Care Worker should possess and demonstrate as part of a therapeutic relationship when working with children/youth: "empathy, genuineness and respect."

1. **Empathy** is the ability to put yourself in other's shoes by trying to understand and relate to the child/youth's feelings, situation and/or motives. Empathy provides the base for the therapeutic relationship and establishes a personal connection.

2. Traits of **genuineness** include being open, honest, and sincere and with an absence of defensiveness and phoniness. This allows the [child/youth] to feel comfortable and allows for more open and honest inquiry and awareness.

3. **Respect** creates the safety that is essential in therapeutic relationships. A CYC Practitioner must accept the child/youth as a whole, which includes strengths and weaknesses. An environment needs to be created where profound issues can be brought to the fore front for examination and transformation.

The Child and Youth Care Practitioner's therapeutic relationship is essential and correlated with positive, successful outcomes for the child/youth. It encourages the clients to share and interact with their CYC Worker in a trusting, meaningful way. It allows them to openly share, without fear, their goals, dreams and wishes. This relationship also allows the child/youth to feel safe expressing their own opinions and desires without feeling they are being judged or having their worker's mandates or agendas imposed upon them (Rodriguez, 2011).

As you can see from above, the three qualities of a CYC that lend themselves to the development of a therapeutic relationship are key to ensuring that you are able to reach your clients in a trusting, respectful manner.

CYC Practitioners must also look at the components of a therapeutic relationship to allow you to stay competent, use professional judgement, act ethically and ensure professional boundaries within the therapeutic relationship.

According to the Ontario Centre of excellence for Child and Youth Mental Health, the foundation of a thereputic relationship is based on trust, respect and power.

1. Trust

Trust is one of the key components when developing a relationship with a child/youth. You need to be able to demonstrate to your client that you have the well-developed skills you need to provide them with quality care and support. They likely have had a history of untrusting and untrustworthy relationships, attachment issues, trauma and abuse, and will look to you to provide a safe environment for them to heal. They are trusting you to have their best interests in mind and your work together will include breaking down any current barriers and then building up a trusting relationship.

Factors that Support the Establishment of Trust

BE EMPATHETIC: you will find that most individual who choose a career in the social services including Child and Youth Care, are empathetic by nature. Because it is your job to help your client feel heard and understood, you will be guiding them and yourself through an abundance of sensitive emotions and discussions. Remember that you will need to balance your emotions, show compassion without pity, be friendly but not their friend, show understanding along with solid common sense.

BE CHILD/YOUTH FOCUSED: Listening skills, both active and passive, are key qualities in a successful Child and Youth Care Practitioner. You are required to stay focused and give your client your undivided attention. As a CYC Practitioner this will serve to allow you to gain insight, make assessments and ultimately develop appropriate interventions and treatment plans.

SET OBJECTIVES: Once you have a clear history and understanding of the child's/youth's story you will begin establishing clear, realistic objectives, based on the needs and issues specifically related to your client. By developing SMART (specific, measurable, attainable, realistic, timely) goals, specific objectives with milestones along the way, including short and long term goals, you will be supporting that child/youth to feel hopeful and look towards their future in a positive light. Keep in mind that no set of objectives is carved in stone, these can be tweaked and adjusted along the way and objectives can be added or removed based on the unique needs of your client.

BE PREPARED: Each interaction with anyone on your caseload should be preceded by preparation on behalf of the Child and Youth Care Practitioner. You should consistently be adding to your skill set and develop your knowledge in order to assist your clients to the best of your ability.

BE FLEXIBILE AND PATIENT: One of the biggest assets a CYC practitioner can possess is the ability to be flexible and patient during the process. In reality, you will come to learn that it is the child/youth who sets the pace with regards to progress, implementation of strategies and behavioural change.

BE FIRM BUT FAIR: Although we may be tempted to coddle a child/youth with whom we are working it is not in their best interest to do so. You will need to learn what motivates the child/youth you are working with and use that to try to maintain positive changes. Keep in mind, however, that progress is not always linear, and your client may require a little push to move forward.

BE PROFESSIONAL: Always remember, no matter how long you work with a child/youth or how close you feel to them, you are a professional. This is why clear boundaries are very important within the Child and Youth Care field. Crossing boundaries can have a serious impact upon the client/practitioner relationship and may become an ethical issue. As a new graduate this can be difficult as you potentially will be close in age to some of your clients. Always remember you are a skilled, trained professional tasked with the responsibility to assist and support the child/youth with whom you are working.

BE UNBIASED: It is your job to leave your biases at the door, so to speak. You should not bring your personal beliefs or preferences to your work with a child/youth. It is your responsibility to be sensitive to each client's heritage, culture, religious beliefs and lifestyle and incorporate those into your work with that individual if it maintains a safe and effective plan for that client.

SEEK HELP: Some of the histories of children and youth that you will work with will be devastating and heart wrenching and complex. You may not have all the skills and expertise to handle every client that comes your way. You will also find, what worked one day for one youth may not work the next day for the same youth. Be sure to reach out and use your colleagues and other professionals in the field, as resources. Don't be afraid to seek support and help from others to better your plan for the child/youth on your caseload.

KEEP CONFIDENTIALITY: As a CYC Practitioner you are bound by your Code of Ethics to maintain confidentiality when it comes to your clients, unless they share information that leads you to believe that they, themselves, their family or others are at risk. If you feel a youth has shared information that you need to report be sure to review your code of ethics surrounding disclosure as well as your individual agency's policies.

Often maintaining confidentiality when working with minors can be very challenging and includes many facets including ethical guidelines, legal guidelines, regulations and clinical judgement. If you ever find yourself in an ethical dilemma that may infringe on your client's right to confidentiality, consult with your colleagues/supervisor as well as the agency guidelines.

2. RESPECT

The second foundation of a therapeutic relationship is respect. This word refers to several things including an expected quality of ourselves and our clients as well as a component of our work.

Regardless of the children, youth and families with which you work, you have the responsibility to respect them as individuals and the responsibility to try to understand them regardless of their differences.

3. POWER

You will always find that there is an imbalance of power within the CYC/child/youth relationship favouring the CYC. The CYC has authority within the system, they have a unique set of skills and the child /youth is dependent upon the service you provide, resulting in a power imbalance innate to this type of work. You are tasked with being aware of this imbalance and using your skills and relationship to create a safe environment for that child/youth.

All of the above are characteristics of a CYC Practitioner that can assist in the development of trust within a therapeutic relationship. They are also cornerstones of what makes and exemplary Child and Youth Care Practitioner.

Professional Boundaries

According to the Ontario Centre of Excellence for Child & Youth Mental Health, a CYC Worker understands that professional and personal boundaries are essential when serving children, youth and families. Boundaries are dynamic and constantly changing when buiding relationships with clients. Practitioners seek objective feedback from sources external to their cases, and they always place "authentic relationships at the forefront of their interactions."

Throughout our lives we are involved in many relationships, with our parents/caregivers, with our siblings, as a student, employee, or customer. Each relationship has its own boundaries that includes what we share about ourselves, our expectation of their behaviour towards us, and our use of personal space, to name a few. These boundaries, distinguish a professional relationship from a personal one, and these boundaries are important when the functions in a professional relationship mimic those of a more familiar role such as that of a friend, parent or sibling, as they can in CYC work.

Establishing a therapeutic relationship and maintaining professional boundaries requires the CYC to understand their distinctly unique role that they play within the life of young people and their families (Davidson, 2009).

Everyone takes personal measures to protect their own privacy. These can evolve and change, depending on our needs at the moment. Usually, we are somewhat resistant to share personal information with new acquaintants, however when a climate of trust and possibly friendship is established we are more likely to share personal information with others. This, is the opposite of a CYC/client relationship.

A CYC Practitioner's relationship with their client is unique because it appears to be the complete opposite of what our natural relationships are like. Children and youth who are working with a CYC Practitioner are hoping to find a safe, trusting environment where they are not judged and are able to find support and assistance to work through their issues.

Clients often enter into a relationship with a CYC Practitioner when emotions are high and they are at their most vulnerable. The expectation is that the client share their most personal thoughts, issues and concerns with a virtual stranger, prior to building a trusting relationship with that individual. Often, because CYC work is time sensitive, it is difficult to quickly build that type of relationships and as noted above, is the opposite of how we naturally build these interactions. Interactions between a client and their worker can often be explosive, volatile and emotional and this is where the skills and temperament of the CYC Practitioner are pivotal in building a therapeutic relationship that is safe and judgement free for that child/youth. However, one must always remember that although you can be friendly with your clients, you are not friends.

It is important to note that a CYC/client relationship is never equal. According to Geldard & Geldard (2005) "regardless of how much effort a CYC puts into making the relationship equal, the CYC will inevitably be in a position of power and influence."

The Professional Relationship Continuum

Davidson (2004) defined the Professional Relationship Continuum as "a basic conceptual framework, which provides both a point of reference and a common language for discussing the actions, choices, and processes related to the boundaries of human service providers' professional relationships."

This continuum refers to a practitioners "attitudes toward emotional connections with, and involvement in the lives of young people and their families in light of the position of trust and power that the professionals are privileged to hold" (Davidson, 2004).

Boundaries are noted on the continuum with extremes at each end being entangled at one end and rigid at the other. The middle of the continuum, balanced, represents the ideal professional, therapeutic relationship that encourages appropriate boundaries and safety for the client.

The professional relationship boundaries continuum

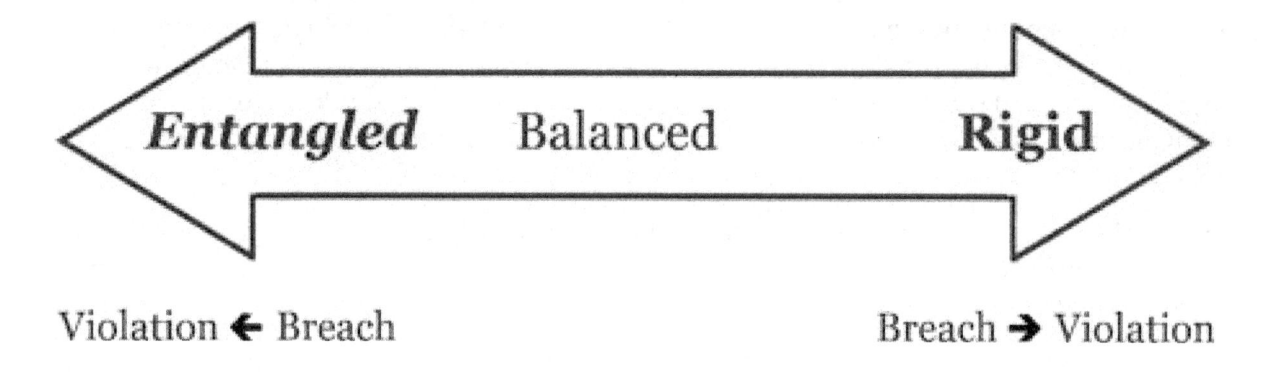

Entangled — Balanced — **Rigid**

Violation ← Breach   Breach → Violation

Looking at the continuum, at its extremes you will recognize that both ends represent the most significant and potentially harmful boundary violations. You will see that the "degree of which a professional's actions are harmful to their client is indicated along the continuum by the terms breach and violation" (Davidson, 2004)

A practitioner who has a genuine and caring manner, who can maintain clear boundaries will demonstrate a balanced practice. You are the type of practitioner who remains aware of your position but does not use it to exploit your client. You will consistently use your professional judgement and self reflective skills while meeting your client's unique and complex needs.

Practitioners with entangled boundaries are unable to step back and reflect upon their work in an honest, subjective manner. They are over involved in the lives of their clients and often invest more of their time, energy and attention of these relationships than others on their caseload.

In contrast, having rigid boundaries involves storming ahead with one's own agenda inflexibly, condescendingly, and/or without attending to the unique and multi-faceted needs of the client. Professionals functioning with such boundaries lack authenticity and sensitivity and exploit the client's vulnerabilities, abusing their position of power as they accentuate the power difference between them.

These descriptions reflect interactions occurring at the extreme ends of the continuum in order to illustrate the differences between the areas of the continuum. It is important to note that the underlying motivations of either extreme may or may not be well-intentioned, and that good intentions may neither counteract nor protect the other person from the impacts of blurred boundaries.

At the other end of the continuum are rigid boundaries. A partitioner with rigid boundaries has little flexibility and often move forward with their own agenda without attending to the multi-faceted needs of their client. CYC Practitioner's that practice in this manner often lack sensitivity and abuse their position of power and often act punitively to demonstrate their power over their clients.

Indicators: What cues can indicate increasingly blurred boundaries?
Extreme boundary violations, such as professional sexual misconduct, occur as part of a process, and are generally the result of incremental steps toward increasingly less balanced behaviors. The process itself crosses boundaries, since any transformation of a relationship that is intended to meet only a professional's needs is exploitative and unethical long before sexual contact has occurred. Sex is simply one possible abusive outcome, remarkable because it is more detectable (Strasberger, Jorgenson and Sutherland, 1992; Fortune, 1995; Irons, 1995; Summer, 1995; Thompson, Shapiro, Nielsen and Petersen, 1995; Colton and Vanstone, 1996). To curtail increasingly blurred boundaries in their own and their co-workers' behaviors, it is critical for professionals to be aware of these incremental steps, which lead to boundary violations.

Indicators of blurring boundaries
The following is a list of experiences and behaviours that may act as warning indicators of increasingly blurring professional boundaries.

Entanglement cues

- Your neutrality is progressively diminishing.
- You reveal information about other clients to this client.
- You reveal information about yourself unrestrainedly.
- You are extraordinarily angered or saddened with this particular client's choices.
- You have intruding thoughts about this client when you are not at work.
- You are unusually invested in changing a client's behaviour.
- You promote a client's dependence on you.
- You encourage a client to separate her/himself from healthy support systems.
- You spend more time with a particular client than usual, in person or on the telephone.
- You meet with a client at the end of day to enable you to extend your time with her/him.
- You meet in uncommon places or in a client's home when it is not necessary to be there.
- You exchange gifts.
- You contrast the satisfying qualities of a client with your spouse/ partner's less satisfying qualities.
- You daydream about a client.
- You long for her/his next visit.
- You plan your attire based on your appointment with her/him today.
- You direct a client in their particular day-to-day details of life.
- You present yourself as the expert on a client's life choices.
- You disapprove of a client's assertive behaviour.

- You act or feel jealous about a client.
- You are defensive when probed about a relationship.
- Physical contact begins.

Rigid cues

- Your neutrality is progressively diminishing.
- You reveal information about other clients to this client.
- You reveal nothing about yourself to a client.
- You feel detached from, or do not care about, a client.
- You are loath to go to work.
- You are unjustifiably pessimistic at work.
- You continue to employ strategies that have been clearly ineffective.
- You are overly intellectual about a client's problems.
- You present yourself as the expert on a client's life choices.
- You are punishing, callous, prejudiced or critical toward a client.
- You use patronizing or derogatory terminology when referring to a client.
- You terminate a conversation in the midst of a client's expression of unresolved emotions because the original time set for the meeting is about to lapse.
- You minimize the degree of pain a client has experienced.
- You are disinclined to exhibit any type of emotion.
- You feel impatient, irritated, or emotionally absent with a client.
- You refuse to offer help to meet a client's needs.

Source: Strasberger et al., 1992; Kowaz, 1996; Davidson, 2000; Texas Medical Association, 2002, cited in http://www.cyc-net.org/cyc-online/cyconline-oct2009-davidson.html

As a professional, you need to be aware of the signs and symptoms and ensure that you are practicing self-care (as discussed in Chapter 12)

As CYC Practitioners we frequently walk a fine line between professional and personal boundaries and presenting as being entangled or not flexible.

To develop a foundation of respect and trust within the therapeutic relationship we must ensure that we are connecting with our client while being conscious of the amount of information, we share with them about ourselves.

CYC has evolved over time and relationships have changed and grown. It is our job as CYC Practitioners to put the child/youth first while taking into account their current situation as well as their history and family make up.

The goal has and should always be putting the child first; however it often takes a tragedy for these strategies to be put in place and for change in practice to occur.

The role of a CYC Practitioner is a very difficult one as we are often only as good as what we are told, and how positive the therapeutic relationship is. Meaning if a child discloses information that indicates they are at risk, we are able to act upon that, however if this information is not disclosed or we have not known the child/youth long enough to recognize the signs, it may be difficult to initially assess the risk that the child potentially could be facing.

Katelynn's Principle

Seven-year-old Katelynn Simpson died in 2008. Her autopsy revealed that she had 70 wounds.

Katelynn's legal guardians had lengthy criminal records and prior involvement with child welfare agencies. The judge who put Katelynn in their care did not know these details. Katelynn's guardians pleaded guilty in 2012 to second-degree murder and are serving life sentences. This is an example of the how the legal and agency systems can fail.

Although it is our goal to always put the child first, this occasionally does not happen due to systemic, legal or agency restrictions. However, due to some tragic results, the Ontario Association of Children's Aid Societies along with the Ministry of Child and Youth Services, changes were made in the form of Bill 57 or Katelynn's Principle.

BILL 89: Katelynn's Principle

This Act was created to serve as a guiding principle for decisions affecting children and the Bill set out guiding principles to direct decisions concerning children (Katelynn's Principle, Bill 89):

- The child must be at the centre of the decision.

- The child is an individual with rights. The child must always be seen, the child's voice must be heard, and the child must be listened to and respected.

- The child's heritage must be taken into consideration and respected. Attention must be paid to the broad and diverse communities the child identifies with, including communities defined by matters such as race, ethnicity, religion, language, and sexual orientation.

- Actions must be taken to ensure that a child who is capable of forming their own views is able to express those views freely and safely about matters affecting them.

- The child's views must be given due weight in accordance with the child's age and maturity.

- In accordance with the child's age and maturity, the child must be given the opportunity to participate before any decisions affecting the child are made, whether the participation is direct or through a support person or representative.

- In accordance with the child's age and maturity, the child must be engaged through honest and respectful dialogue about how and why decisions affecting them are made.

- Every person who provides services to children or services affecting children is a child advocate. Advocacy may be a child's lifeline and it must occur from the point of first contact and on a continuous basis thereafter.

As Child and Youth Care Practitioners, Katelynn's Principle should act as a guide for all of our interactions with our clients within a therapeutic relationship and beyond.

Chapter 10 - Let's Reflect

As a CYC practitioner how will you ensure that you stay balanced in your practice and ensure you have appropriate therapeutic relationships with your clients?

Chapter 10 – Worksheet

Choose the best answer and explain your choice.

1. You are walking down the street and see a client

    You:

    a) Ignore your client

    b) Nod hello

    c) Stop and chat

    d) Other:

2. Your phone is broken and your client needs to be able to contact you

    You:

    a) Provide your personal number

    b) Tell your client to call the office and leave a message

    c) Say your phone is broken

    d) Other:

3. Your client asks to borrow your book.

    You:

    a) Give your client the book

    b) Suggest they join the local library

    c) Offer to lend him/her the book

    d) Other:

4. A client asks you if you are married and if you have children

    You:

    a) Tell your client the truth.

    b) Tell him/her it's not an appropriate question

    c) Show family photos

    d) Other:

6. A client praises you

    You:

    a) Thank your client and say that they are special too

    b) Explain that you are just doing your job

    c) Tell your client that those kinds of compliments are not appropriate

    d) Give him/her a hug

    e) Other:

7. You are working with a client who is flirting with you

    You:

    a) Say thank you and hoping it won't happen again

b) Tell your client that your relationship is a professional one

c) Refer your client to someone else

d) Other:

9. One of the clients invites you to a party

You:

a) Attend, just this once

b) Tell your client that it is not appropriate for you to attend

c) Say you will try and then don't show up

d) Other

Source: Adapted from "How tight (or loose) are your professional boundaries?" Published September 10, 2009 edition of Community Care Magazine.

Chapter 11 – Checklist

☐ I understand what a therapeutic relationship is

☐ I am aware of professional boundaries

☐ I understand the components of trust, respect and power

☐ I am aware of the Professional Relationship Boundary Continuum

☐ I understand the need for confidentiality and when I have a duty to report

☐ I am familiar CYC with the Code of Ethics

☐ I feel confident in my ability to create a positive therapeutic relationship with healthy professional boundaries

References and Resource

Community Care Magazine. (2009). "How tight (or loose) are your professional boundaries?" Community Care Magazine.

Davidson, J. (2009). Where do we draw the lines? Professional relationship boundaries and child and youth care practitioners. CYC-Net, 128(October). Retrieved from https://cyc-net.org/cyc-online/cycol-1201-anglin.html

Geldard, D., & Geldard, K. (2005) Basic personal counselling: A training manual for counsellors. NSW, Australia: Pearson Education.

Ontario Centre of Excellence for Child & Youth Mental Health. Retrieved from https://www.cymh.ca/en/index.aspx

Rodriguez, M/ (2001). Essentials of the therapeutic relationship. Posted on April 1, 2011 9:23 am. Retrieved from https://www.ccpa-accp.ca/essentials-of-the-therapeutic-relationship

Rogers, C. (1951). Client-centered Therapy: Its Current Practice, Implications and Theory. London: Constable.

Chapter 8: What is Evidence-Based Practice and Treatment Models

Real Life Story

A referral was received from a source that advised the agency her neighbour's 7-year-old son had set fire to his bedroom which subsequently rendered their home temporarily uninhabitable.

The family was placed with friends and the agency became involved due to some red flags that the fire department brought to the attention of the Child Protection Worker.

They shared, that upon their arrival at the scene, the mother was very verbally abusive and aggressive with her young children, they also noted that the undamaged part of the home was in disarray, dirty, with several liquor and beer bottles strewn about.

Upon further investigation it was determined that there were further concerns that required involvement of Child Welfare Worker. The child was removed from the care of his mother, and placed with a family member, based on the severity of concerns that was determined through a risk assessment completed by the Child Protection Worker.

During interviews with the child, it was determined that he was from a single-family home, often left unsupervised and corporal punishment was used as a discipline method. The child further reported that his mother had "many boyfriends" and there were often strangers frequenting his home.

The agency became involved for a long period of time to assist and support the mother and child to help mitigate the circumstances surrounding his fire setting behaviour. There are many further details that were involved in this file, however, after a prolonged period of treatment, support, evidence-based intervention (TAP-C, CBT) the family was eventually reunited and the child is doing well, with ongoing professional support.

According to the TAP-C program, Juvenile firesetters have been more likely to experience home lives that are characterized by marital discord, inappropriate parent–child relationships, parental alcoholism, parental rejection, and poor in-home supervision than non-firesetters (Becker et al., 2004; Hill et al., 1982; Kolko & Kazdin, 1990; Sakheim & Osborn, 1986).

What is Evidence-Based Practice?

Evidence-based practice, as defined by the Child Welfare Information Gateway, "involves identifying, assessing, and implementing strategies that are supported by scientific research. Child welfare agencies are increasingly aware of the need to focus their resources on programs that have demonstrated results."

> In 2008, The Ontario Society for Children's Aid Society's completed a survey to explore the ways in which front-line CYC practitioners understand and use EBT (Evidence Based Treatment) and EBP (Evidence Based Practice), as well as to describe the scope of practice of CYC practitioners in group care programs.
>
> The results of the survey show that:
>
> - Interventions used by CYC practitioners are theoretically linked to EBTs and have demonstrated positive outcomes for children, youth and families.
> - Procedural manuals for implementing and evaluating these interventions in group care need to be developed in most programs.
> - Residential group care programs do demonstrate an understanding of EPT and EBP and many programs following standardized case planning procedures.
> - EBP is implemented differently in various sectors that provide residential services for children and youth. Implementation of EBP is affected by "funding, access to information, and educational preparation of front-line workers. There were differences in these factors between children's mental health and child welfare programs as well as among the private children's residence programs."
> - Further research is required "to demonstrate the specific connections between group care models, CYC practitioner interventions and client outcomes." This would foster the ability to replicate EBT models in group care.
> - Further research is required to demonstrate the relationship between practitioner interventions and client success.
>
> **Source**: Ontario's Association of Children's Aid Societies

What is Life Space Intervention?

Life space intervention is the use of daily events as a therapeutic opportunity. These events can occur in a residential setting or family setting, wherever the CYC shares a life space with their client.

This method acknowledges the potential for communication between the CYC practitioner and their client that they share through life experiences.

Daily events are considered and explored by the CYC practitioner to help their client gain an understanding of their life experiences and how they can impact their future experiences. This understanding facilitates the foundation for intervention that will help the youth obtain control and understanding over their environment.

According to Graham (2003), life space intervention can intervene in two ways. First, "emotional first aid on the spot: is an intervention that aids the mastery of tasks necessary to progress through the developmental stages of childhood and adolescence. The second, is called "clinical exploitation of life events." Here the practitioner focuses on daily life events to help children and youth to understand their past and present behavioural experiences and to prepare them to live independently.

According to Reclaiming Youth at Risk (2021), Life Space Crisis Intervention (LSCI) is a therapeutic strategy that uses crisis situations as opportunities to affect change and allow children and youth to discover alternate patterns of behaviour.

This method blends different interventions, such as psycho dynamic, cognitive, behavioural and pro social methods, to facilitate powerful teaching moments and teaching interventions as they occur within their own life space.

Relational practice is committed to creating equitable and inclusive space for children and youth that promote the ethics, values and morals of the Child and Youth Care profession.

At the centre of relational practice, is the life space. This concept has evolved over time and the main focus that has been maintained is that there is a very strong focus on "place". The field of Child and Youth Care is committed to meeting youth **where they are at** regardless of where this may be within a regional, cultural or emotional context. This essentially involves meeting where their lives unfold (Gharabaghi & Stuart, 2014).

The majority of the evidence-based practice theories and methods can and should be used in the "life-space" of the child, whether that be within the context of residential care, family system or school based, to name a few.

10 Evidence-Based Treatment Models

There are several identified practice/treatment models recognized as being evidence-based. The 10 most frequently identified are:

1. Cognitive Behavioural Therapy (CBT)

Cognitive behavioural therapy is a time sensitive, structured, present oriented psycho-social therapy that has been proven to be effective I supporting many mental health issues and behavioural concerns by identifying goals and providing assistance and strategies to overcome themCBT focuses on challenging and changing unhelpful cognitive distortions and behaviours, improving emotional regulation, and the development of personal coping strategies that target solving current problems.

The tools deployed in CBT—which include learning to identify and dispute unrealistic or unhelpful thoughts and developing problem-solving skills—have been used to treat a broad range of mental health challenges. CBT is now considered among the most efficacious forms of talk therapy, especially when clients incorporate strategies into their daily life. This effort to gain insight into one's cognitive and behavioral processes and modify them in a constructive way often involves ongoing practice, but is favored by many clients as it can require fewer therapy sessions than do some modalities (Psychology Today, 2021).

2. Therapeutic Crisis Intervention (TCI)

Also known as the abbreviation TCI is a crisis management protocol developed by Cornell University for residential childcare facilities. The purpose of the TCI protocol is to provide a crisis prevention and intervention model for residential childcare facilities which will assist them in:

- Preventing crises from occurring
- De-escalating potential crises
- Effectively managing acute crisis phases

- Reducing potential and actual injury to children and staff
- Learning constructive ways to handle stressful situations
- Developing a learning circle within the organization

3. COPE Creating Opportunities for Personal Excellence

COPE is a province wide, community mental health service offering support to adults aged 16 and older, with emotional and/or mental health concerns. COPE accepts referrals from a wide variety of community sources. Self-referrals are welcome.

Also, under the umbrella of COPE is ConnexOntario:

> "Bridging the child/youth and adult mental health systems, ConnexOntario has collected information on more than 700 on- and off-campus mental health programs available to Ontario's postsecondary students. ConnexOntario is also involved in several key initiatives aimed at the postsecondary education sector including the Good2Talk Helpline, the CICMH initiative, and the For Students, by Students mobile application project.
>
> **Postsecondary Mental Health Initiative**
>
> ConnexOntario, along with various partners, is involved in an initiative to create a service to address the addiction and mental health concerns of Ontario's postsecondary student population. This service will address current service gaps for students through innovation, information, engagement, and education and support postsecondary providers with information on services throughout Ontario.
>
> **Good2Talk – Ontario Postsecondary Helpline**
>
> Operated by four partners including: ConnexOntario, Kids Help Phone, Ontario 211 and the Ontario Centre of Excellence for Child and Youth Mental Health; Good2Talk is a toll-free, and confidential helpline funded by the Ontario Ministry of Training, Colleges and Universities. Good2Talk offers Ontario's postsecondary students professional counselling, mental health and addictions information, and connections to local resources. The Good2Talk services are available to students 24/7/365, in both English and French.
>
> In addition to providing students with information regarding on-campus supports (from financial aid offices and sexual health centres, to ombudsman and counselling offices), Good2Talk is able to provide referrals to hundreds of off-campus services, including mental health and addiction services, housing supports, and legal and community health services.
>
> ConnexOntario and Good2Talk are integrated: ConnexOntario provides the information and referral component, ensuring that accurate and timely information regarding mental health and addiction programs and services that can be accessed in Ontario."

Source: https://www.connexontario.ca/

4. SNAP – Stop Now and Plan

SNAP®, which stands for Stop Now And Plan, is an evidence-based cognitive behavioural model that provides a framework for teaching children struggling with behaviour issues, and their parents, effective emotional regulation, self-control and problem-solving skills.

The primary goal of SNAP is to help children to stop and think before they act, and keep them in school and out of trouble.

Did you know...

- An estimated 14% of Canadian children experience mental health issues
- Conduct problems are the most referred mental health issues in children under 12
- Approximately 60% of incarcerated males have a history of conduct problems
- It costs approximately $110,000 per year to keep a youth in a secure custody facility in Canada
- It is estimated that future costs for a career criminal will be $1,143,604 if no early intervention takes place
- In contrast it costs approximately $6,000 for a child and their family to participate in a SNAP program
- Children aged 6-12 are good candidates for learning self control strategies

Source: https://childdevelop.ca/snap/about-snap

5. CPI – Crisis Prevention Institute

Nearly 40 years ago, Gene J. Wyka Sr., Gene T. Wyka, and AlGene Caraulia Sr. created a model for crisis prevention and intervention. They drew from disciplines such as kinesics, psychology, physiology, and communication to create Nonviolent Crisis Intervention® training.

They began to teach mental health professionals how to stay safe and keep patients safe during times of crisis.

Currently, the Crisis Prevention Institute offers various programs based on the needs within the field. These include:

- Verbal Intervention
- Non-violent Crisis Intervention
- Non-violent Crisis Intervention; Advanced Physical Skills
- Specialize renewal

6. Brief/Solution Focused Therapy

Brief/Solution focused therapy is unique in that it does not focus on historical events as many therapies do, it focusses on finding solutions and strategies in present time and the goal is to find a quicker resolution to one's issues/concerns. This approach provides coaching, support and questioning to find the most appropriate solutions that the client is capable of implementing.

Brief/solution focused therapy can be used with other intervention methods or can stand alone. It is effective with children and adults and can assist with various types of issues, including, but not limited to: behavioural problems, family issues/dysfunction, abuse, addiction and relationship issues (Psychology Today, 2021).

7. Positive Parenting Program-3 P

Triple P, Positive Parenting Program, is a program that is used in supporting families that provides strategies to assist them in preventing social, emotional behavioural and developmental problems in children. By enhancing parents' knowledge, skills and confidence, Triple P can assist parents in creating and developing coping strategies and behavioural programs while focussing on their individual needs. Triple P is based on the social learning theory along with cognitive, developmental, and public health theories. There are 5 intervention levels that are designed to build on each other in intensity and individuality to meet each family's specific needs.

8. TAP-C- fire/arson prevention

TAP-C , The Arson Prevention Program, is a program that was created to reduce the risk of fire setting among children and adolescents.

This program will identify children who are at risk setting fires and will make appropriate education and counseling available to them.

9. Goldstein's Social Skills

There are many programs that are in existence or that can be developed to address issues with regards to social skills in children and youth. Goldstein's social skills is just one program that has a history of successful outcomes when dealing with interpersonal conflicts, teaching self control, anger control, moral reasoning and pro-social behaviour.

10. Pharmaceutical interventions

Often, certain diagnoses that result in negative behaviours require pharmaceutical interventions prescribed by an appropriate medical practitioner.

These 10 practices have evidence to support their value and results and are often successful when used alone or in conjunction with each other. However, they are not the only evidence-based practice theories or models available to Child and Youth Care Practitioners.

Additional practices also used include, but are not limited to:

Psychosocial outpatient treatments:

- includes structured counseling, motivational enhancement, case management, care-coordination, psychotherapy and relapse prevention.
- day programs are often an alternative to residential treatment, if the child/youth meets the criteria for treatment

Family-focused treatments:

- Family-focused therapy uses a combination of two approaches to therapy, including psychoeducation and family-oriented psychotherapy. FFT treats the whole family unit (i.e. both parts of the couple, the entire family, etc.), as having a family member with mental health or behavioural issues, can hugely impact the entire family (as a unit and as individual members) (Jarrold, 2019).

Integrated community-based treatment:

- integrating services to screen, prevent, diagnose and treat all chronic conditions and mental illness by creatively using technology and optimizing the roles of all members of the multidisciplinary team

School-based interventions:

- specific theoretical approaches and classroom application of intervention
- how the unique skills, abilities, and support offered by the Child & Youth Worker can contribute to the social, emotional, and academic growth of students.
- forming partnerships with teachers, school administration, and other professionals

Does Evidence-Based Practice Always Work?

This question is considered in the following excerpt from an article by John Stein and published on the website CYC-Net:

> If professionals rely too heavily on evidence-based practice, they might not be providing the best possible service for the children and families with whom they work. Indeed, it is possible that they may be contributing to some other problems. Some children might need something in addition to an evidence-based intervention, or something entirely different.
>
> Consider children who have serious problems with temper control. There are numerous cognitive behavioral interventions that have been shown to have merit. Should one of these interventions eliminate the problem, all is well. Should such an intervention reduce outbursts from several times a week to only a few times a month, what then? Obviously, the intervention has had a beneficial effect. Do we stop here? Are we finished? Have we done all that can be expected? All that is necessary? Are two or three tantrums a month acceptable?
>
> Do we have a child who so misunderstands his social environment and the motivations of others that he perceives a serious threat where none exists, becoming so enraged so quickly at times that he is unable to employ self-control techniques that he seemed to have mastered? Do we have a child who has learned that it is wrong for her to become angry and then feels that she deserves to be punished for allowing herself to become angry?
>
> Or do we have a child who is chronically angry? A child for whom anger is a mood? A child who successfully suppresses a pervasive anger most of the time, until for some reason defenses fail, releasing pent up rage that is out of all proportion to what is happening in the moment.
>
> Do we need to provide some education and experiences in social situations in addition to cognitive behavioral interventions? Do we need to provide specific therapies? Do we need to provide something else? A safe environment? Relationships with caring, understanding people? A little hope? Or something else entirely?
>
> Before qualifying as evidence-based practice, interventions are no more than someone's informed decision about what might work. Many such interventions do not make it into the literature, no matter how effective. Some professionals simply do not have the time or the resources to conduct a study, write it up, and submit it for publication.
>
> Evidence-based practice may be indicated, perhaps even necessary at times. It may not always be sufficient. Professionals should never allow evidence-based practice to limit their goals, objectives, creativity, or innovation. Rather, they should continue searching and innovating based on their knowledge and understanding not only of human development and behavior in the social environment but also of the children with whom they work and the environments in which those children live, to achieve the outcomes they both seek. Individual children and the social environments in which

they live are too complex to rely on one-size fits all prescriptions. We should not rest until we have achieved success.

The evidence that matters is not the evidence from some study. The evidence that matters is the evidence from the children with whom we work. It doesn't matter how well the intervention did with someone else's kids in some other setting. The important evidence is how the intervention works for the kid or kids with whom we are working.

But we must be careful, even with this evidence. We should not conclude that we have found the answer just because the evidence shows that our intervention contributed to some incremental change that proves to be statistically significant using some statistical analysis. Reducing temper tantrums from several per week to two or three per month is indeed significant. It is not sufficient. We need to look further.

So, should we rely on evidence-based practice? I think we should always consider using evidence-based practice. I don't think we should rely on it too heavily. We can and should do more. Our children and families deserve our best.

Source: https://www.cyc-net.org/cyc-online/cyconline-dec2009-stein.html

Children who have mental health needs may come to the attention of professionals in schools, primary care offices, welfare systems, or detention facilities. The fragmentation of the mental health service system means that for evidence-based practice to reach those who provide care to children, a range of training curricula, materials, and approaches must be developed and specifically tailored for the providers in these systems (Kimberly, Hoagwood, Burns, Ringeisen and Schoenwald, 2001).

Chapter 8 - Let's Reflect

To help us reflect on this chapter, let's take a look at the discussion threads from CYC-Net (2010) posted by Thom Garfat and Leon Fulcher.

For a number of years now we (the field) have been referring to a Child and Youth Care (CYC) Approach. A typical list of characteristics associated with this approach might include:

- Being with people as they live their lives
- Pro-activity in intervention
- Responsive practice
- Intentionality of action
- Counselling on the go
- Developmentally appropriate intervention

- Hanging Out with people
- Hanging In – good times and bad
- Doing With, (Not For or To)
- Strengths-based focus
- Engagement & Connection as a foundation
- Being in Relationship and the relational
- Needs-based focus in planning and intervention
- Interventions focused on the present
- Flexibility/Individuality of Approach
- Family engagement
- Focus on Context of interaction and intervention
- Attention to Meaning-Making
- Attention to, and use of, rhythmicity
- Self awareness and the use of self (It's All About Us)
- Use of daily life events as a focus for intervention

As a CYC practitioner, how might respond to the following questions?

1. Are there characteristics, based on your experience in the field (working, workshops, reading, etc.), which you think should be added to the list because you find them appearing frequently in the field? If so, what are they? And where have you seen them?

2. Are there characteristics, based on your experiences, which you think should be eliminated from the list? If so, what are they, and why?

3. Are there characteristics, based on your own personal values and beliefs, which you think we should be trying to incorporate into our approach? If so, what are they?

Source: https://www.cyc-net.org/threads/characteristics.html

Let's Reflect continued...

Chapter 8 – Worksheet

1. Define evidence-based practice.
2. Define and explain life space interventions and provide an example.
3. List the 10 evidence-based practice models listed in this chapter.
4. Provide a definition and example for 3 of the models you listed for question #2.
5. Explain the 4 additional models discussed in this chapter.
6. Provide an example of each using resources from your home community.

Chapter 8 – Checklist

- [ ] I understand what is meant by evidence-based practice
- [ ] I have an understanding of what is meant by life space intervention
- [ ] I am familiar with/or will expand my knowledge of the 10 evidence-based practice methods outlined in the chapter
- [ ] Cognitive Behavioural Therapy (CBT)
- [ ] Therapeutic Crisis Intervention (TCI)
- [ ] COPE Creating Opportunities for Personal Excellence
- [ ] SNAP – Stop Now and Plan
- [ ] CPI – Crisis Prevention Institute
- [ ] Brief/Solution Focused Therapy
- [ ] Positive Parenting Program-3 P
- [ ] TAP-C- fire/arson prevention
- [ ] Goldstein's Social Skills
- [ ] Pharmaceutical interventions

I understand the following practices:

- [ ] Psychosocial outpatient treatments
- [ ] Family-focused treatments
- [ ] Integrated community-based treatment:
- [ ] School-based interventions
- [ ] I recognize the need for on-going reflection with regards to treatment planning and practice
- [ ] I understand that evidence-based practice is not the only plan or strategy used for treatment of children and youth

References and Resource

Child Welfare Information Gateway. (2931). "Evidence-based practice". Retrieved from https://www.childwelfare.gov/topics/management/practice-improvement/evidence.

Gharabaghi, K., & Stuart, C. (2014). Life-space Intervention: Implications for Caregiving. Retrieved from https://reclaimingyouthatrisk.org/courses/life-space-crisis-intervention/

Graham, G. (2003). The use of life space intervention in residential youth care. European Journal of Social Education. pp. 33-34. Retrieved from https://www.cyc-net.org/profession/readarounds/ra-graham2.html

Hoagwood, K., Burns, B.J., Kiser, L., Ringeisen, H., and Schoenwald, K. (2001). Evidence-based practice in child and adolescent mental health services. Psychiarty Online. Retrieved from https://doi.org/10.1176/appi.ps.52.9.1179

Jarrod, J. (2019). What is family focused therapy and how is it used in treatment for bipolar disorder? Retrieved from https://www.therapytribe.com/therapy/what-is-family-focused-therapy/

Psychology Today (2021). Retrieved from https://www.psychologytoday.com/us/basics/cognitive-behavioral-therapy

Root, C. and Mackay, S. (2007). The link between maltreatment and juvenile firesetting: Correlates and underlying mechanisms. Child Abuse & Neglect, 32(2): 161-76. DOI: 10.1016/j.chiabu.2007.07.004

Stewart, C. and Saunders L. (2008). The role of child and youth care practitioners in evidence - based practice in group care: Executive summary. OACAIS Fall 2008, Volume 52 (4).

Chapter 9: Why Include Family and Significant Others in the Planning for Children and Youth?

Real Life Story

Two little girls (aged 1 & 2) were brought into care due to their parent's substance abuse. They were placed in a foster home together. The parents did not exercise their access and eventually all access was suspended.

Approximately 2 months after the girls came into care, the agency received a phone call from a woman claiming to be their maternal grandmother. She and her family wished to care for the girls in her home. Following a complete assessment, the maternal family was approved to care for the girls.

As part of the assessment, it was determined that the grandparents did not even know about the grandchildren until a family friend informed them.

The grandparents struggled with their decision as they knew the girls were settled into the foster home and were attaching to the foster family. However, they felt very strongly that the girls should be with family due to the connections and permanency they could provide.

The Importance of Family

According to the Ontario Association of Children's Aid Societies, in the fiscal year 2019 – 2020, there were almost 9,300 children and youth in care based on a monthly average. This means that 9,300 children and youth were not placed with their family members, unless under a Kinship Care agreement.

Unfortunately, being in care can result in negative outcomes such as low academic achievement, homelessness or unstable housing, frequent involvement with the criminal justice system, increase in mental health issues, and experiencing deep loneliness and lack of connections.

The damage is caused by several moves to multiple homes with multiple foster families. The youth do not experience any stability, cannot feel secure or form positive attachments. These are the foundations that every child and youth need to be successful.

In Ontario, 82% of youth in care are diagnosed with some special needs and 46% rely on psychotropic medications to help manage them (Our Voice Our Turn, 2012). Approximately 33% of Crown Wards suffer with some form of mental health issue.

What options are we able to offer to children and families at risk, apart from bringing the children into care? Statistics have proven, time and time again, that children fare better when raised by kith or kin versus being raised within the foster care system. As a result, the inclusion of families is now common in Child and Youth Care practice (Shaw & Garfat, 2004; Garfat, 2001). However, this was not always the case.

A review of program descriptions from the middle of the last century (e.g., Ohio, 1941; Redl & Wineman, 1952) determined that programs were mainly focused on the young person. The family was commonly viewed as the problem, and thus not involved in treatment planning, and were essentially unaware of the status of their child. Today, however, families are seen as the part of the solution and staff are "expected to engage with the child and their family" (Milligan & Stevens, 2006, p.103).

Maintaining Family Relationships

Family describes many things and has many meanings. Family can be your biological origins or a support system that you create that includes significant people in your life.

> "It is evident from the changing nature of programs and the growing volume of national and international literature, that the future client of the Child and Youth Care worker will be the family, the whole family, as research demonstrates both the effectiveness and efficacy of total family involvement. Indeed, it is more common today to think of even residential care as a resource for families."
>
> (Stuart & Carty, 2006)

When we think of "family" we traditionally imagine a mother, father, and children, however, families have evolved and look very different than they did in the past. Regardless of their composition, it is the emotional connection, the shared heritage and the understanding of the history that makes family so vital in planning for children and youth.

Research (Helton, 2011) shows that children placed with a family fare better psychologically, emotionally, socially, and interpersonally compared children placed in foster care or group care.

Everyone, especially children, need long lasting relationships to grow and develop. According to (Park & Helton, 2010) children who have a consistent, stable and nurturing environment, which fosters attachment and relationships, can develop positive and healthy adult relationships. This environment and bonds are critical especially when a child or youth leaves care. It is this love and guidance that will support them.

Kin/Kith Options

Kinship is close, long-lasting social relationships that surround us. In terms of child and youth care, kinship is understood in terms of nurturing and protection of a child by their family and relatives. Kin provide stability, safety, family connections, culture, and history. Similarly, kith includes friends, neighbours and significant others who are part of a person's cohesive group.

When a child or youth is no longer able to stay with their primary caregiver, it makes sense to place children with their kin and kith. As such, kin and kith are options mandated by legislation. Kinship placement allows the child to live with people in their web of social relationships and extended family members, which allows for family and cultural preservation.

The Child Welfare Information Gateway identifies different types of kinship placements such as Kinship Service, Kinship Care, and Customary Care. The assessment and training requirements may be different depending on the type of placement. For instance, compared to Kinship Service, the in-care placement assessment is much longer and more intrusive for the family and can involve licencing requirements, monthly payments to assist with the costs of caring for the child, and supports from the placing agency. Below you will find further information on the different forms of kin/kith care.

Customary care is a kinship placement within the Indigenous community where the Band and the appropriate child welfare agency are involved in the best placement for the child.

What is Kinship Service?

Individuals who are biologically related to a child are referred to as kin. Individuals who are not biologically related but have a significant connection to a child such as stepparents, friend, teacher, godparent, coach, neighbour are referred to as kith. Both kith and kin can be considered to care for a child who has been removed from their primary caregiver's care. When a kith or kin placement occurs, it is referred to as Kinship Service if the child is placed with an approved caregiver but has not been brought into care by the agency. Essentially Kinship Service is an out of care placement, with family or friends that is assessed, approved, supervised and monitored by the child welfare agency. In order for a child to be placed in a Kinship Service home, the agency must receive consent from the primary caregivers. If the caregivers do not provide consent, and the agency feels that it is the best interest of the child to be placed, or remain in the kinship placement, the Society can deem the Home a Designated Place of Safety and obtain a supervision order placing the children in the kin placement. For this period of time, the child is considered "in care" of the Society. Once the Place of Safety has been approved the child can be removed from care but remain in the kinship placement. This is an important piece to note as the standards for children in care differ from those out of care, therefore, for the period of the Place of Safety Designation the child and the kin home must meet Child In Care Standards.

A Kinship Service placement allows the child to remain in a family/friend environment where their history, heritage, culture and traditions are honoured and understood. This allows for feelings of security, safety and belonging.

What is Kinship Care?

As mandated by the CYFSA, kinship options are always explored for children who are in need of protection. Kinship Care requires that a child/youth to be brought into care but placed with an approved kinship caregiver. A child/youth may temporarily be placed in a foster or group home, until the Kinship Care assessment is completed and approved. As with Kinship Service, Kinship Care allows the child to remain connected with their family and provides a sense of safety, security and belonging for the child.

A Kinship Care home is essentially an approved foster home, although the caregivers are family/close friends (kith). The child welfare agency is the legal guardian of the child, however, the Kinship Caregivers are responsible for the day to day care of the child.

A Kinship Service home assessment/placement is the least intrusive and the preferred placement for the child as it allows them to be supported by the agency but not in the care of the Society. However, due to certain circumstances such as the needs of the child, the financial status of the caregivers, and the level of required supervision by the agency, it may be determined that a Kinship Care placement is the best and safest option for the child.

To be approved as a kin/kith in care caregiver, the Society involved must complete a SAFE home study (Structured Analytical Family Evaluation). This is a Ministry mandated home assessment that is completed by all foster, adoptive and kin in care caregivers. It is an extensive and in-depth assessment of the individuals who are planning to care for a child/youth. They will also be required to attend PRIDE training (Parenting Resources Information Development and Education) which is a 9 week, ministry mandated program to assist prospective kin caregivers in preparing to care for a child who may have experienced trauma, neglect or emotional, physical, and sexual abuse.

Once a Kinship Care family is approved, the Child in Care standards apply to the child/youth placed in that home, and the family is required to meet all expectations and licensing standards of an approved foster home. The child in care standards includes the mandate that a permanent plan/placement for a child under 6 must be determined within 1 year of the child being placed into care; and within 2 years if a child is over 6.

This differs from kinship service in that due to the fact the child is not in the care of the agency, these standards do not apply. Kinship Service caregivers are still required to participate and complete a thorough assessment and be approved prior to a child being placed in their care. However, because the child is not in the care of the agency the licensing standards of kin in care or foster care, do not apply. However, kinship service caregivers are requested to consider a permanency plan for the child/youth.

What is Customary Care in Ontario?

"First Nation, Métis, and Inuit (FNMI) family structures differ from the typical nuclear family in Western culture. FNMI families have strong family values, are often extended, and share collective responsibility towards children. FNMI families may be related by blood, but can also be tied by clan or other social structures. This collective responsibility for raising children is known as customary care" (OACAS, 2020).

In 1985, the CFSA recognized Customary Care in relation to FNMI families involved with a child welfare agency; the CYFSA has expanded on this Act.

Customary Care refers to individuals caring for a child/youth of Aboriginal descent, who is not the child's parent or primary caregiver as per the child's band or native community.

Indigenous beliefs are such that they foster a strong sense of community and cultural identity and are essential in the formation of lifelong relationships. Based on those beliefs it is felt by the FNMI community that placement within a customary care setting is the most beneficial for Indigenous children and youth and will allow them to continue to be immersed in their cultural heritage.

Two Types of customary care

Customary care is intended to be short term placement of Indigenous children with caregivers, within their community, to allow the parents/primary caregivers to heal.

1. Traditional Customary Care

A traditional Customary Care agreement can be entered into without the involvement of a child welfare agency. It can be an agreement entered into by the child, their primary caregivers, the customary caregivers and the band.

2. Formal Customary Care

A formal Customary Care agreement differs in that it does involve a child welfare agency and the agreement is a legal arrangement involving the Band, primary caregivers, customary caregivers and the child protection agency. In a Formal Customary care placement, child in care and foster care standards and licensing are applicable.

Traditional or Formal Customary care allows children of Indigenous descent to be supported by their community while maintaining their cultural heritage, family traditions and connections (FCS Renfrew Country, 2020).

Supporting Cultural Heritage

It makes sense to assume that the family who is caring for a child, would be of the same heritage as that child, however, this is not always the case. Due to the ever changing face of the "family," different family systems, cross cultural relationships, same sex relationships as well as personal choice, not all family members share the same cultural heritage as that of the child.

The key purpose of the CYFAS is to promote and protect the well-being of children. We understand that a child is grounded in their own culture. Thus, the Act was expanded to ensure recognition of various forms of diversity such as "race, ancestry, place of origin, colour, ethnic origin, citizenship,

---

Jordan's Story

Jordan River Anderson was a First Nations child from Norway Cree House Nation in Manitoba. Born in 1999 with complex medical needs that could not be treated on-reserve, he spent more than two years in a hospital in Winnipeg before doctors agreed that he could leave the hospital to be cared for in a family home. However, because of jurisdictional disputes within and between the federal and provincial governments over who would pay costs for in-home care, Jordan spent over two more years in hospital unnecessarily before he tragically died in 2005. He was 5 years old and had never spent a day in a family home.

Jordan's Principle

In response to this tragedy, Jordan's Principle was created. It is a child first principle calling on the government of first contact to ensure First Nations children can access public services on the same terms as other children. In December 2007, Motion-296 in support of Jordan's Principle passed unanimously in the House of Commons. If the federal and provincial governments followed Jordan's Principle, there would be no jurisdictional disputes, and First Nations children would not get caught in the middle of government red tape, like Jordan did.

Source: First Nations Child & Family Caring Society of Canada

family diversity, disability, creed, sex, sexual orientation, gender identity and gender expression" (CYFSA, June 1/17).

How to support kinship/customary care placements

When children are placed with alternate caregivers the focus is for permanency for that child, be it with the caregivers, the agency or reunification with the parents. Reunification is the preferred outcome and through several methods, child protection agencies provide concurrent planning platforms to ensure the plan is in the best interest of the child, while including the child/youth and their families in the planning process.

ADR/FGC (Alternate Dispute Resolution/Family Group Conferencing)

Family Group Conferencing (FGC) is one form of Alternate Dispute Resolution (ADR) that is recommended as an initial step when trying to resolve differences and facilitate planning for a child who is no longer able to reside with their primary caregivers. This is the first measure to plan for the child and potentially settle differences and create a cohesive plan that will allow the family to avoid having to attend a court hearing (ADR-Link, 2020).

A Family Group Conference Co-ordinator will be assigned to the file and will arrange for a family conference. A "conference" is a technical term for a meeting attended by a child's kith, kin, and CAS representatives (i.e., CAS, Kinship Worker, and CYC). A conference is organized by a FGC Coordinator, who is understood to be independent and neutral. Participation in a meeting is voluntary (ADR-Link, 2020).

The conference can include anyone in the child's life who can support the child and their family with the goal of reunification or an alternate permanent plan. It can also include the CAS worker, his/her supervisor, the kinship worker and the CYC who is supporting the child/youth.

Prior to the formal conference, the FGC Co-ordinator meets one-on-one with all members who have agreed to participate in the conference. The facilitators explain the FCG procedures and protocols to the participants individually to ensure their understanding and commitment to the process.

When the conference begins, there are three parts to the process (ADR-Link, 2020):
1. information sharing
2. family private time
3. agreement plan

The conference begins with the information sharing meeting. This is when the agency shares their concerns for the family and the family has the opportunity to share their hopes for the meeting and for the child/youth. The family listens to CAS concerns for the child's safety. There may also be input from other professionals and service providers. During this process, family members are able to raise questions and comment. The CAS workers present their "bottom lines," which are the required plans to ensure the safety of the child and to facilitate family connections and potential reintegration of the child/youth with their primary caregivers.

In the next phase, the family and their kith and kin have time to meet privately to discuss and create a child safety plan. All "professionals" or agency related individuals leave during the family time of the conference. The goal of this time is for the family to create a safety plan for the child/youth and their family that is in the best interest of the child/youth while also supporting their primary caregivers, if possible.

This can include anything from family offering to support the child's current placement or provide an alternate placement, supervising the primary caregivers during visits or arranging regularly scheduled visits with the child/ren to ensure the maintenance of family connections. It can also include supporting the primary caregivers in attending treatment, medical appointments or therapy. The main goal is for the family to support and facilitate their final plan which allows for less involvement of the agency. This also supports the belief that the family knows the child best.

In the final phase a plan is agreed upon. Everyone returns to hear the family's plan. The plan has to meet the criteria outlined by the CAS. If the "bottom lines" are met and the plan is deemed safe, then the plan is accepted. The Society will monitor the plan to ensure continued safety of the child, however, the organization and participation is the responsibility of the involved family members (ADR-Link, 2020).

Signs of Safety

The Signs of Safety® is a strength-based, safety-organised approach to child protection casework. Andrew Turnell and Steve Edwards created this approach based on their work with over 150 front-line statutory practitioners. The Signs of Safety has gained international attention as is used in North America, Europe and Australia.

Many child protection agencies across Canada have adopted the Signs of Safety model and use it in their practice. The Signs of Safety model includes tools and strategies to work with families, and acknowledges that families know their children the best.

The Signs of Safety approach uses several tools to work through the process with families and children and as CYC practitioners you will likely have more exposure to the tools specific to children which are highlighted below.

The Signs of Safety

The Signs of Safety uses a strength based approach to planning and includes strengths, worries, hopes and plans by asking questions such as; what's working well?, what are we worried about?, how worried are we? What needs to happen? This is documented on a template referred to as the 3 columns.

When we think about the situation		
What are we worried about?	What's working well?	What needs to happen?
HARM/DANGER Statements	Existing Strengths Existing Safety	Safety Goals Next Steps

On a scale of 0 – 10 where 10 means everyone knows the children are safe enough for the child protection authorities to close the case and 0 means things are so bad for the children that they can't live at home; where do we rate this situation?

1 _____ 10

The Signs of Safety risk assessment process integrates professional knowledge with local family and cultural knowledge, and balances a rigorous exploration of danger/harm alongside indicators of strengths and safety.

Source: https://www.signsofsafety.net/what-is-sofs/

Three Houses

The Three Houses method mimics the three key assessment questions of the Signs of Safety Framework:

- What are you worried about?
- What's going well?
- What needs to happen?

By using child friendly illustrations and language, a CYC will guide the child/youth through the process to determine their feelings, thoughts and needs.

The Fairy/Wizard

The Fairy/Wizard tool is similar to the Three Houses Tool, but uses a drawing of a fairy or wizard to explore the same three questions. It is often used with preschool and early primary school aged children because they are familiar with these images (Nottingham City Council, Signs of Saftey Resource).

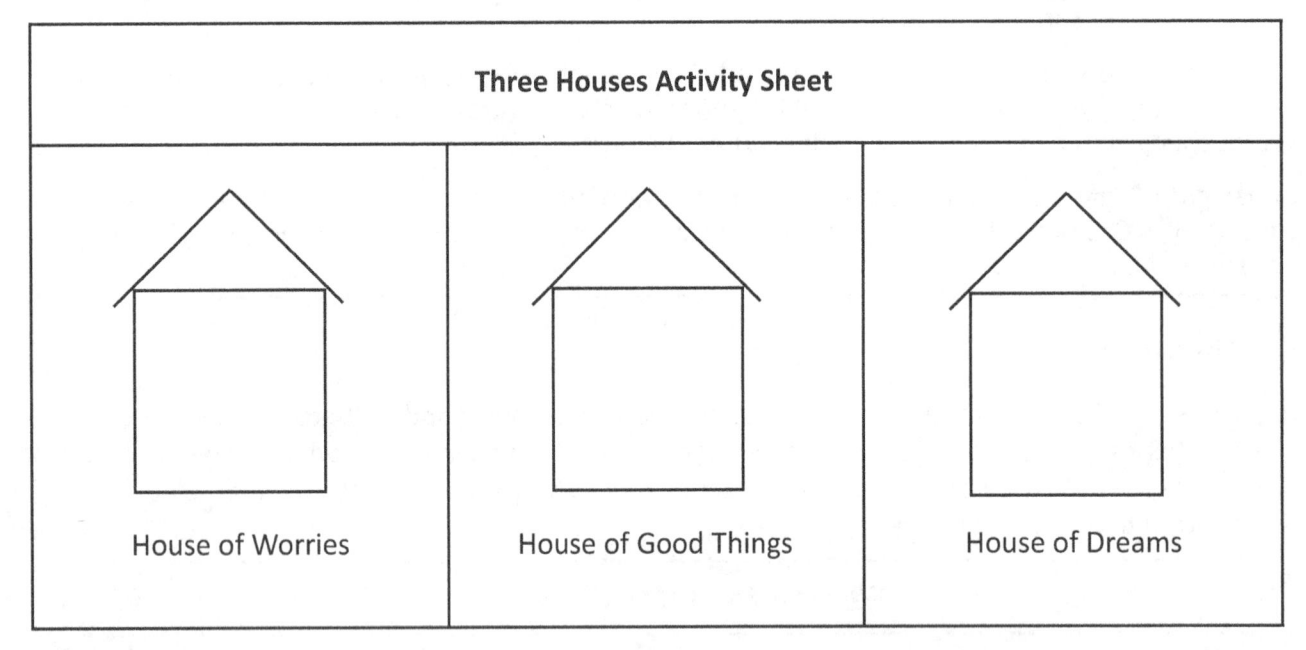

Three Houses Activity Sheet

| House of Worries | House of Good Things | House of Dreams |

Safety House

The "Safety House" is a visual tool designed to include children in safety planning and to hear their views on what their family should do to keep them safe in their homes. Children can also identify the roles the adults should take in order to support safety, people they don't feel safe with, rules of the saftey house, people who live in the house, and people who visit (Partnering for Safety, 2020).

Words and Pictures

The "Words and Pictures" method helps children understand their current situation and what has happened in their family. By using words and pictures, family members and professionals collaborate to build a storyboard. The storyboard is also used to help children, family members, and support workers to understand why child protection is involved with the family (Partnering for Safety).

The process, procedures and policies of child welfare are always evolving based on the needs of the children we serve. However, one constant is that families are crucial to a child's development, support system, heritage, and wellbeing.

Family is often the single most important influence in a child's life. From their first moments of life, children depend on parents/primary caregivers and family to protect them and meet their needs. Parents and family form a child's first relationships. Children thrive when parents are able to actively promote their positive growth and development. However, when a family is unable to meet a child's needs, for various reasons, extended family members can provide a safe, nurturing environment that have the ability to support their history, heritage and cultural beliefs. Although child welfare is always evolving and changing to best meet the needs of the children, youth and families they serve, one constant is that family is pivotal to a child's positive growth and development and overall wellbeing.

Chapter 9 – Let's Reflect

If you were working with a child who was going to be placed with kith/kin, what would you look for in that family to ensure the child's needs are being met?

Chapter 9 - Worksheet

1. Discuss why family is so important to maintain a child's heritage and identity?

_____
_____
_____
_____
_____

2. Define Customary Care and discuss the two subtypes:

_____
_____
_____
_____
_____

3. Describe your understanding of ADR/FGDM.

_____
_____
_____
_____
_____

4. Discuss the Signs of Safety model and share your opinion of the tools that support its practice.

_____
_____
_____
_____
_____

Chapter 9 – Checklist

- ☐ I have an understanding of the definition of family.
- ☐ I recognize the changing face of the family
- ☐ I understand what kinship mean
- ☐ I understand what kith means
- ☐ I know the difference between kin service and kin care
- ☐ I understand the two types of Customary Care
- ☐ Traditional

- ☐ Formal
- ☐ I understand the purpose of the Signs of Safety tools for children
- ☐ 3 Columns
- ☐ 3 houses
- ☐ Wizards and fairies
- ☐ Safety house
- ☐ I understand why it is important to maintain a child's cultural heritage

References and Resources

Canadian Medical Association Journal (CMAJ). 2009 Dec 8; 181(12): E265 E266. doi: 10.1503/cmaj.091968

Child, Youth and Family Services Act, 2017. Retrieved December 28, 2020, from https://www.ontario.ca/laws/statute/17c14

Customary care. Family & Children's Services of Renfrew Country. Retrieved December 28, 2020, from https://www.fcsrenfrew.on.ca/services/child-welfare/research-quality-assurance/

Family group conferencing. ADR-Link. Retrieved December 28, 2020, from http://adr-link.ca/wp-content/uploads/2016/05/FGC-INFO-w-letterhead.pdf

Garfat, T. (2001). On the development of family work in residential programs. *Journal of Child and Youth Care, 14*(2), iii-iv.

Helton, J., (2011). Children with behavioral, non-behavioral, and multiple disabilities, and the risk of out-of-home placement disruption. *Child Abuse & Neglect, 35*, 956-964.

Jordan's principle. First Nations Child & Family Caring Society. Retrieved December 29, 2020, from https://fncaringsociety.com/jordans-principle

Milligan, I., & Stevens, I. (2006). *Residential child care: Collaborative practice*. London: Sage.

Park, J.M., & Helton, J. (2010). Transitioning from informal to formal substitute care following maltreatment investigation. *Children and Youth Services Review, 32*, 998-1003.

Shaw, K. & Garfat, T. (2004). From front line to family home: A youth care approach to working with families. In T. Garfat (Ed.), A *child and youth care approach to working with families* (pp. 39-54). New York: Haworth.

Stuart, C., & Carty, W., (October, 2006). *The Role of Competence in Outcomes for Children and Youth: An Approach for Mental Health*. Toronto: Ryerson University.

What is customary Care in Ontario? Ontario Association of Children's Aid Societies. Retrieved December 29, 2020, from http://www.oacas.org/childrens-aid-child-protection/permanency

What is signs of safety? Signs of safety. Retrieved December 28, 2020, from https://www.signsofsafety.net/what-is-sofs

Chapter 10: How to Engage Families in Your Practice

Real Life Story

A youth and her single mother were not getting along. The youth was acting out, missing curfew, skipping school, being disrespectful and oppositional, and her mother was unable to manage her behaviours and keep her safe. It was agreed upon between the local child protection agency, the youth and her mother, that they would enter into a temporary care agreement where she would be assessed and a treatment plan would be entered into that involved both mother and child.

The youth entered into the TCA and complied with all the requirements, she attended counselling, she was respectful of the staff, she regularly attended school and began to re-build her relationship with her mother.

Her mother was to attend parenting teens classes and counselling to assist her in parenting her daughter. The mother attended classes sporadically and did not attend counseling, however, the staff noticed a marked improvement in the relationship between the youth and her mother. When the TCA was complete it appeared that the relationship was on a positive trajectory and the youth was returned home.

However, due to the fact that the mother did not consistently attend the parenting classes and did not attend counselling, she quickly reverted to her old ways of parenting. Although the youth tried to use her new found skills to manage her home situation, without the support of her mother, she was unable to do so, and subsequently reverted to her old behaviours. Tensions escalated within the family unit.

The sad part of this story is that the youth ended up aging out and was unable to be brought back into the care of the society.

CYC Approach to Family Work

In the previous chapter we discussed the importance of including family in planning for their children and youth. This chapter will discuss how to do this while maintaining a client focused approach.

In the past, a family potentially would hand their child over to the experts to "fix" them and then encourage their return to the family once the "fixing" was complete. However, this method has proven to be ineffective due to the fact that the child/youth was being returned to the environment that contributed to creating the undesirable behaviours. If the environment remains unchanged, regardless of gains made by the child/youth, it is unlikely that the changes will be supported by the family. Therefore, engaging families in planning, treatment and caring for their child/youth is paramount to a successful outcome.

When you begin to work with families, you will likely use treatment or program plans that were developed for individual children. When a family becomes involved the individual plans need to have a family focus. These plans need to reflect the values and beliefs of the family. If you want to work with a family, you have to shift your focus to include the family on a daily basis (Fulcher & Garfat, p. 90).

The theoretical basis for Child and Youth Care is the creation and maintenance of the therapeutic relationship from within the life space of the client. All other intervention strategies and theoretical applications are secondary to the creation and maintenance of this vital element (Phelan, 2003). The reality of Child and Youth Care family work is that the majority of clients do not initially want practitioners to be involved in their lives, having had interventions imposed upon them by societal intervention rather than resulting from individual assent.

The Child and Youth Care approach to family work means "being with [families] while they are doing what they do. It means the utilization of daily life events as they are occurring for therapeutic purposes" (Garfat, as cited in Shaw & Garfat, 2003, p.43). The "being with families" approach also supports and acknowledges that the families are the experts on their own children and that families should parent their own children. The behaviour of your client is essentially anchored within the family resulting in what needs are being met by your client.

This type of information will be gathered through your observations of, and interactions with, the family within their life space. Having this perspective will assist you in formulating and implementing intervention strategies that are specific to each family's needs (Jones, 2007).

Child and youth family care work represents a powerful therapeutic intervention method.

CYC Practitioners generally do not graduate prepared to enter into family work, however, much of their practice involves the family. Therefore, it is crucial to develop skills that will enable you to do positive, forward thinking work with not only children and youth, but with their families as well.

Who is Your client?

As a CYC practitioner you will engage in building caring interactions with youth, who find it hard to create attachments. You will work to foster safe, trustworthy connections for youth to learn and grow.

Often in the first two years of their career, CYC professionals face a tough choice between "blaming" parents and families and "rescuing" the youth, or viewing parents and families as in need of support so they can better handle life's challenges (phelan, 2003). This experience is important for a CYC to successfully learn to manage family work. The worker develops respect for parents who are dealing with very challenging behaviour. A skilled worker understands how to use a "developmental lenses" and theories to support the youth (phelan, 2003).

Parents will recognize if their family support worker has the experience necessary to deal with youth. This experience builds credibility and trust with the family.

A key lesson for a worker is to understand that destructive patterns of living are hard to change and the challenge is to facilitate change. Building a strong relationship with the family is essential to affecting change. The worker may encounter resistance to relationship building and has to understand that it is a normal part of human behaviour (phelan, 2003).

A CYC engaging in family support work must use the family's life space and lived moments to create interventions. Using lived experience is strategic, immediate and purposeful. This type of intervention allows the CYC Practitioner to facilitate shifts and changes that may not occur using less direct or passive methods. During family work, it is important to recognize and acknowledge that the parent is the expert on their family and the family must be able to see that the CYC respects this relationship.

According to Fulcher and Garfat (2015), there are 25 characteristics of a Child and Youth Care approach that are applied to working with families. They are listed below with a brief description.

1. Participating with people as they live their lives:
   - As a CYC Practitioner you will immerse and involve yourself in all aspects of the daily life of your clients and families
   - At the centre of the CYC approach is the ideal that if changes are made in behaviours through the course of everyday, real life situations, then change will be more enduring

2. Rituals of encounter:
   - This requires a CYC Practitioner to be mindful and give conscious thought with regards to the way you engage with others, especially the families with which you work
   - This includes, but is not limited to paying attention to a family's culture, traditions, lifestyle and history while remaining respectful and educating yourself in areas that will benefit the family

3. Meeting them where they are at:
   - This involves engaging with families where they live in their lives
   - It means accepting them for how they are and who they are as we encounter thee

4. Connection & Engagement:
   - If connections with your clients and their families are not overall positive experiences there is a risk that the interventions and strategies presented will not be effective
   - Being connected and developing positive relationships with your clients and families is the basis of child and youth care. Without this connection the family's engagement will be lacking

5. Being in a relationship:
   - Not to be confused with having a relationship, 'being in a relationship' means interacting with a person at a deep meaningful level which impacts both the young person and their helper

6. Using daily life events to facilitate change:
   - Using real life moments as they occur within a family provides the most powerful and relevant opportunities for families to learn and make changes

7. Examining context:
   - Involves a conscious awareness of how everything that occurs for and with this young person and their family does so in a cultural socio-economic context that is unique to a particular place and to the history of the family members who live there

8. Intentionality:

   - It is important that the work a CYC Practitioner engages in is done with purpose and intentionality
   - You will find that there are few random acts of intervention and that usually they are planned carefully to fit with the established goals that have been determined between yourself and the family

9. Responsively developmental practice:

   - Knowing the child/youth well enough to understand their developmental ability and tailoring your plan with such considerations in mind. In this process the capability of the family members must also be considered
   - Instead of reacting to behaviour CYC Practitioners respond pro-actively in a manner consistent with a young person and their family's developmental capabilities and needs

10. Hanging out:

    - It can appear to those not in the field that a CYC Practitioner does everyday things with a child/youth/family, however, all of these "simple" things are relevant and extremely important
    - During times of "hanging out" you are building relationships of "trust, safety, connectedness and intimacy"
    - It is from a place of safety that the family, as a system, might explore opportunities for modifying boundaries and re-aligning family sub-systems

11. Hanging In:

    - Throughout your career there will likely be many times as a CYC Practitioner that you feel you may want to give up. One of the main characteristics of a CYC Practitioner is tenacity and the ability to rise to the challenge
    - Through your work and presentation you will demonstrate commitment and caring for the child/youth and family
    - Through this process, you help to build hope for the future

12. Doing "with", not "for" or "to"

    - Individuals learn better when they are engaged in the process, therefore, it is important not to "do" things "for" or "to" your client. Your goal is to help them learn to do things independent of your presence
    - The intent is "being and doing *with* others"

13. A needs-based focus:

    - The purpose of a CYC Practitioner is to meet the needs of the family and family members
    - The family is stronger when their needs are met as a family

14. Working in the now:
    - It is important to focus on the present, which assumes that "we are who we are, wherever we are"

15. Flexibility and Individuality:
    - Every family you work with is unique, what may work today may not work tomorrow, therefore it is imperative that you remain flexible and create your plans to suit each individual within the family
    - Each intervention you present to a family should be specific to that family member as you understand them
    - One size does NOT fit all

16. Rhythmicity:
    - Refers to the shared experience of engaging synchronized, dynamic connection with another or others
    - CYC Practitioners are encouraged to pay particular attention to rhythms that ripple throughout the family's life, in their interactions with friends, teachers, carers, and between family members – strengthening rhythms of connectedness, belonging and caring

17. Meaning-making:
    - This is a process that a family will go through to try and make sense of their experience with you and to have it be meaningful in their family and behaviours
    - Practitioners must always be mindful of the impact their interventions and involvement with their clients will have on the family as a whole

18. Reflection:
    - Involves thinking about one's work
    - Part of your reflection should always include assessing how your personal history or biases may be influencing your work at any given moment

19. Purposeful use of activities:
    - The use of activities facilitates learning and supports young people to explore new experiences in a safe environment with their family

20. Family-oriented:
    - While practitioners work one-on-one with a client, their impact on that individual extends to the family. It is "family work"

21. Being emotionally present:
    - Being present remains a central feature of child and youth care practice
    - This involves allowing one's self to be in the moment

- Family work challenges the practitioner to be emotionally present with multiple others, who have many needs, often at the same time
- Being in the present is integral to CYC practice
- You must allow yourself to be in the moment and use these moments to continue to assess your interventions and strategies all the while providing support to you client and their family

22. Counselling on the go:
    - "Often CYC work happens through fragmented interactions, often referred to as "life-space counselling"
    - These moments of connected interaction are often more powerful than traditional approaches to "talk therapy""

23. Strengths based and resilience focus:
    - Using a strength based approach to build on positive behaviours will enable you to strengthen the family relationships
    - Developing strengths and nurturing positives will help a family to prepare for life challenges

24. Love:
    - Pay attention to love in the family. Love can provoke powerful experiences

25. It's all about us:
    - Who you are as a practitioner influences other people
    - Being self aware can help you practice in the best interest of others
    - Your work with families should be "holistic, ecological and inclusive"

Source: CYC-Online October 2018

Parenting Support

The Child and Youth Care approach to working with families allows you to create experiences that encourage the family to revisit maladaptive behaviour patterns and beliefs, and enables you to work with them in their own life space to modify, or change these behaviours or patterns.

Using the 25 characteristics of a Child and Youth Care approach listed above, you can create strong family connections, facilitate change and encourage new and modified interactions among all members.

Parent Education Programs

A parent education program is a course that helps to improve a person's parenting skills. These courses cover common issues parents encounter and specific issues that affect infants, toddlers, children and teenagers.

According to Wilder Research (2016), the benefits of parenting education can improve parental skills, confidence, practices, mental health and well-being, It can build social networks and parent-child interactions. It can also provide alternatives to punishment and lower the risk of child abuse.

Wilder Research (2016) lists some best practices in parenting education. These include engaging parents, reaching parents early, adapting programs based on cultural differences, offering frequent sessions to reinforce learning and routines, and to use trained parenting educators.

Many agencies offer parenting support in the form of group work and meetings. These may vary by regions or location, however, one such program, Triple P (Positive Parenting Program)(as mentioned in Chapter 8), which is recognized worldwide as one of the most effecting parenting programs. It is used in countries all over the world and has won numerous international awards.

Triple P is based upon knowledge of child psychology and best practice. This evidence based approach is continually measured and refined. It is applicable on a large scale to reach whole populations, while being adaptable to individual family situations.

The original program consists of parenting groups for parents with children and teens. There are 3 seminars for parents of children up to 12 years: The Power of Positive Parenting; Raising Confident, Competent Children and Raising Resilient Children. The programs for children and teens is offered in several formats including group, one-on-one help, seminars, and online support.

There are also specialized Triple P programs including Stepping Stones Triple P (for parents of children with a disability), Lifestyle Triple P (for parents of children who are overweight), Family Transitions Triple P (for parents going through divorce or separation) and Indigenous Triple P (for Indigenous families).

More often than not, it is CYC Practitioners who take the training and facilitate the program delivery due to their specialized education, knowledge of children and youth as well as their commitment to supporting and helping families.

In an article written about the fundamental process of intervention with working with high-risk adolescents and their families (Ballantyne, Macdonald & Raymond, 2008), it is reported that little attention has been paid to fundamental generic components of family-worker interaction and service provision that are necessary for successful interventions.

Their findings indicate that a positive therapeutic relationship based on trust and respect is critical to effective interventions. In addition, a number of factors related to service were found to be important, such as flexible hours, prompt response to requests for help, and services that are culturally relevant and sensitive.

It has been determined that one of the key indicators of success when working with adolescents at risk is the quality of the relationship between the youth and the service provider. Even though future intervention methods may prove successful, research has shown that if the therapeutic relationship is not a positive one, long term changes may not occur. Trust and respect have been determined to being pivotal in the development of a positive therapeutic relationship, which can be developed through an on going process of understanding, listening and acknowledging and caring for the individuals and families with whom you work.

Building a trusting relationship is challenging and requires ongoing support. Forms of support that are beneficial include peer support, training and development, relief from challenging situations, debriefing, and supervision (see (Bradley, 1996; Light, 1996; Mathews, 1996; Nicoloff & Watson, 1996).

The most helpful services and programs are those that are accessible. To be accessible, families require services that have flexible hours and are close to home, easy to find, immediate, available in 'natural' settings, and culturally relevant.

Service providers can assist families to set goals by having the youth and family define the issues. They can help families to set goals to address risks and to set clear and realistic goals. They can help to get everyone on board with meeting the goals, and they can assist with developing a plan to address any issues.

At the heart of any successful intervention, regardless of the method or technique employed, is the therapeutic relationship. Those things that support and build this alliance between the worker and the family are critical to successful work with high-risk adolescents and their families (CYC-Net, 2008).

Chapter 10 – Let's Reflect

- When you think about what drew you to the CYC profession did your vision include family work?
- Why or why not?
- How do you plan to incorporate families into your daily practice?

Chapter 10 - Worksheet

1. T or F

CYC work is solely about the youth

2. T or F

Including a family in planning for a youth is pivotal for success

3. T or F

As a CYC Practitioner the youth is your only client

4. T or F

CYC practice has always involved family members

5. T or F

It is necessary to possess all 25 characteristics listed in this chapter to be an effective CYC Practitioner

6. T or F

The key to any successful intervention is a positive therapeutic relationship

Chapter 10 – Checklist

- [ ] I have an understanding of, or have practiced, the following characteristics of working with families as a CYC Practitioner
- [ ] Participating with People as They Live Their Lives
- [ ] Rituals of Encounter
- [ ] Meeting them where they are at
- [ ] Connection & Engagement
- [ ] Being in relationship
- [ ] Using daily life events to facilitate change
- [ ] Examining context
- [ ] Intentionality
- [ ] Responsively developmental practice
- [ ] Hanging out
- [ ] Hanging In
- [ ] Doing "with", not "for" or "to"
- [ ] A needs-based focus
- [ ] Working in the now
- [ ] Flexibility and Individuality

- ☐ Rhythmicity
- ☐ Meaning-Making
- ☐ Reflection
- ☐ Purposeful Use of Activities
- ☐ Family-oriented
- ☐ Being emotionally present
- ☐ Counselling on the go
- ☐ Strengths based and resilience focus
- ☐ Love
- ☐ It's all about us

References and Resources

Ballantyne, M., Macdonald, G., and Raymond, I. (2008). Fundamental processes for interventions: Working with high-risk adolescents and their families, 110(April). Retrieved from https://cyc-net.org/cyc-online/cycol-0804-interventions.html

Garfat, T. (1995, 1998). From front line to family home: A youth care approach to working with families. In T. Garfat (Ed.), *A child and youth care approach to working with families* (pp. 39-53). Binghamton, NY: Hawthorn Press.

Garfat, T., Freeman, J., Gharabaghi, K., and Fulcher, L. (2018). Characteristics of a relational child and youth care approach revisited. *CYC-Net,* October. Retrieved from https://www.cyc-net.org/pdf/Characteristics%20of%20a%20Relational%20CYC%20Approach%20Revisited.pdf

Jones, Lahn. (2007). Articulating a Child and Youth Care approach to family work. *CYC-Net,* 104 (September). Retrieved November 5, 2020, from https://cyc-net.org/cyc-online/cycol-0709-jones.html

Phelan, Jack. (2009). Child and youth care family support work. *CYC-Net*, 120(February). Retrieved November 5, 2020, from https://cyc-net.org/cyc-online/cyconline-feb2009 phelanchapter.html

Shaw, K., & Garfat, T. (2003). From front line to family home: A youth care approach to working with families. In T. Garfat (Ed.), *A child and youth care approach to working with families* (pp. 39-53). Binghamton, NY: Hawthorn Press.

Wilder Research. (2016). The benefits of parenting education: A review of the literaure for the Wilder Parent Education Center. Retrieved from https://www.wilder.org/sites/default/files/imports/LitReviewSummary_10-16.pdf

Chapter 11: What are Burnout and Vicarious Trauma and How Do I Manage Them?

This chapter is an adaptation of Best Start Resource Centre. (2012). When Compassion Hurts: Burnout, Vicarious Trauma and Secondary Trauma in Prenatal and Early Childhood Service Providers. Toronto, Ontario, Canada: author.

> **Real Life Story**
>
> A worker attended a home where it was alleged that the residents were using drugs, engaging in loud verbal arguments, and leaving their baby unattended. Upon arrival to the residence, the worker observed several cars in the drive way and noted that there were several people sleeping throughout the house. There was a strong smell of smoke and marijuana and drug paraphernalia was strewn all over the coffee table in the living room.
>
> The referral source mentioned concerns about a child; however, the worker searched the home and was unable to find a child in plain sight. She continued to search the home and came across an old play pen with a pile of blankets in it. When she moved the blankets, she found a young child. The child looked to be gray and immobile and the worker was concerned that the baby had passed away. The child's pallor was gray, and his eyes were closed and his lips were blue. His diaper was full and wet, and he had sores all over his body. When the worker reached into the play pen, the baby opened his eyes and stared blankly.
>
> The child was brought to a place of safety, and with care and support began to thrive, however, thoughts about the child continued to invade the workers mind. She seemed unable to control them or to manage her emotions when they arose.

As Child and Youth Care Practitioners we consciously take on the responsibility of being involved in the most challenging aspects of people's lives. Our job is to provide support to individuals and families who are struggling with abuse, addiction, mental health issues, neglect, domestic violence and ongoing behavioral issues. We work in this field of practice because we have aspirations to provide professional guidance and want to master the skills that are required to support children, youth and their families during their times of crisis and uncertainty. Oddly enough, the role of a child and youth care practitioner has its own set of potential hazards that may impact the well-being of the worker. It is essential for us to be aware of these hazards to assure that we can bolster our own well-being and in turn the wellbeing of our clients.

Within the child and youth work practice there are attributes that make child and youth care practitioners notably defenceless. It is not uncommon for people who practice in the helping field to have a sense of empathy towards the families with whom they encounter. Throughout their schooling, child and youth care practitioners are taught that they have the ability to bring about successful outcomes with the families that they work with. It is no wonder that so many child and youth care practitioners create unrealistic expectations towards their own influence when working with families. Factors beyond the control of child and youth care practitioners make it difficult to practice regular and consistent self-care. For example, organizations may establish impractical expectations for workers to manage large and complicated caseloads.

Having a clear understanding of the distinctions between terms that explain the impact of stress and trauma on child and youth care practitioners is essential. The following terms and concepts will introduce you to the potential impact on service providers.

Burnout

Burnout can be thought of as a mental, physical and emotional collapse that is caused by prolonged exposure to stress or stressful situations. Burnout is generally correlated with the work environment and tends to present itself when the work setting lacks support, caseloads are high and there is a lack of empathy by management towards frontline workers. Burnout does not present itself after a single stressful situation or event. It is usually an accumulation of smaller stressful situations that eventually take their toll on the person. If not addressed, burnout can impair decision making and possibly lead to fractured relationships between the worker and client, the worker and peers or the worker and management/supervisors within the work environment. By utilizing self-care techniques, maintaining healthy relationships, scheduling time for breaks and lunches and by feeling supported by management/supervisors, you can dramatically reduce the risk of burnout. Some signs and symptoms include:

- Alienation from work related activities
- Physical symptoms such as headaches or stomach aches
- Emotional exhaustion
- Reduced performance
- Lack of sleep
- Fatigue

Vicarious Trauma

Vicarious trauma can be defined as the emotional residue that is left over after working with a child, youth, adolescent or family for an extended amount of time. Consistent exposure to a client's traumatic and stressful experiences will at times evoke feelings of exhaustion, isolation, and poor mental health. Comparable to burnout, vicarious trauma is something that manifests itself over time. Vicarious trauma is a feeling of anxiousness and engrossment of the experiences that clients relay to their counselors.

As a Child and Youth Practitioner, you should make yourself familiar with the signs and symptoms of vicarious trauma and the side effects of working with clients who have experienced trauma.

What to look for:

- Insomnia (trouble sleeping)
- Lack of motivation
- Irritability
- Binge eating

- Lack of interest in activities you once enjoyed
- Low self esteem
- Feeling you haven't done enough for your clients
- Feeling overwhelmed with your workload
- Constantly worrying about your workload

Not only can vicarious trauma impact a Child and Youth Practitioner's personal life, it can also cause difficulties in the person's work environment as well.

- What to look for:
- Dropping out of work committees
- Avoiding interactions with peers
- Tardiness
- Refusal to participate in agency events
- Poor communication
- Poor interpersonal relationships
- Taking frequent sick days (due to work stress)
- Frequent job changes
- Poor judgement

Risk Factors

Risk factors fall into several categories:

Individual Risk Factors	Work Risk Factors	Community Risk Factors
Personality and coping style	Role at work	Culture
Current life circumstance	Work setting and exposure	Resources at large
Social supports	Work conditions	Community factors
Spiritual connection and Resources	Agency support	
Work style	Affected populations responses and reactions	

Individual Risk Factors

1. Personality and coping style

Throughout our lives we develop an individual coping style based on our exposure and experience. What presents as triggers for some may not represent a trigger for others. Our individual coping styles can change to adapt to the situation.

2. Current life circumstances

Our life circumstances constantly change and therefore our coping strategies must change along with them, however, this is not always the case. We often rely on old mechanisms for new problems and discover that our strategies are no longer effective. We need to be conscious of not allowing our day-to-day stressors and hassles to interfere with our objective work as CYC practitioners. We also must be patient with ourselves as change can take time.

3. Social Supports

To be resilient, we require support; we cannot do everything on our own just as we don't expect our clients to work in a vacuum. Having a loving, depdendable, reliable support system that we can turn to during times of stress or distress can provide us with balance, harmony and context. Stress and pain are often exacerbated if we do not have a positive, accessible support system or resource options available to us.

4. Spiritual connections and resources

Often when people find themselves in times of distress, strain or traumatic situations, they turn to a belief in a higher power, whatever that means for the individual. It has been demonstrated that individuals who have a spiritual dimension to their wellness experience have a higher level of resilience that supports them through trauma and difficult times.

5. Work Style

Every individual has a personal work style, which affects your susceptibility to burnout and vicarious trauma. If your work style is valued, supported and respected in the work place, you will likely be at a lower risk for burnout and vicarious trauma. However, your susceptibility can heighten if your work style is in conflict with the policies and procedures of your agency, co-workers and managers.

Work Risk Factors

1. Role at work

Depending on your role and responsibilities at work, your risk factors for burnout and vicarious trauma can increase. Some concerns that place individuals in a higher risk category can include, but are not limited to: a new employee, unclear expectations, level within the company and associated responsibility, your happiness within your assigned role, and your level of stability within your role and agency.

2. Work setting and exposure to trauma

Depending on your role and responsibilities, you may be exposed to different situations and experiences than someone else with another role within the same agency. For example, CYC's who work in a hospital setting will have completely different experiences than those who work in the school system, residential treatment or child welfare. One of the most important factors related to the onset or continuation of burnout and vicarious trauma is directly related to the type and duration of trauma. This can be exacerbated by a heavy caseload and a supervisory style that does not support or reflect your work style.

3. Environmental Conditions

The health and growth of an individual, family, organization or a community is influenced by six environmental conditions:

1. Safety
2. Belonging

3. Consistency/Predictability

4. Opportunity

5. Acceptance/Love

6. Hope

It is difficult for a person to reach their full potential when one or more of these conditions is absent or has been compromised.

4. Agency and supervisory support

How supported we feel by our co workers and superiors, as well as the overall treatment of staff, is extremely important when difficulties present themselves. When staff are exposed to clients who have been traumatized or feel traumatized themselves, a supportive agency is key in the processing of this situation. The best evidence-based strategy with regards to the management of vicarious trauma is reflective practice. You will note that reflective practice is a key component in every aspect of child and youth care.

Community Risk Factors

1. Culture

Further risk factors can be related to culture. You must ask yourself if there are issues with language, ethnicity and belief systems. You may often find yourself in a situation where a cultural practice and values may conflict with those of western practice or the practices of your agency. You need to ask yourself the following questions when assisting clients to avoid confusion, triggers and misunderstandings:

- Is English their first language? If not, is a translation service available?

- What brought them to your country and more specifically to their current circumstance?

- What are the cultural norms that may impact your relationship with your client or their sharing of their story with you?

- As a worker, are you able to put aside you own biases and world views to effectively work with a diverse caseload?

2. Community Resources

As CYC practitioners we often rely on community resources and other agencies to support our plans for our children, youth and families. These agencies can often provide basic needs such as housing, employment and food. As we know, the social service system is bogged down and the wait lists are lengthy. It can be very distressing for a families and workers to experience the lack of support for their clients.

Reducing Risk

As a practitioner it is always our job to reduce risk factors for our clients. With regards to burnout and vicarious trauma, we must take a proactive versus a reactive approach wherever possible, to potentially avoid more significant issues in the future. As an individual and member of an agency there should be protective factors that guide and support your work. It is important that an individual approach be taken within an agency that involves protecting workers against vicarious trauma and supporting their recovery if exposed.

These protective factors can be individual such as your level of self awareness, ability to reflect, awareness of your strengths and weaknesses, ability to seek support and guidance, and your ability to identify and react to stressors and pressures early.

It is imperative to recognize that you are not working alone and to frequently check your feelings and reactions and ask for help when necessary. Everyone needs a support system.

The ability to balance your work, school and home life is pivotal in reducing the risk for burnout and vicarious trauma. Everyone needs an outlet for reflection and self care. Finding balance is a key protective factor for all practitioners.

Self care is pivotal for CYC practitioners to remain happy and healthy in their chosen careers. This can include a variety of activities such as exercise, hobbies, volunteering, yoga and meditation. Allowing daily time for relaxation and reflection is extremely beneficial. Always remember that in order to effectively care for others you must be able to care for yourself.

Organizational Protective Factors

We rely on our employers to provide us with the tools, policies, procedures and appropriate supports to allow us to do our job safely and effectively. Creating a culture of safety, consistency, acceptance and belonging are all key protective factors for any agency. If your employer does not offer these and you are unable to obtain them elsewhere, you are at a greater risk for burnout and vicarious trauma. A supportive and safe work environment is essential.

Part of being a supportive employer is the ability to identify those employees who are struggling. Many practitioners who are suffering from stress or vicarious trauma may not recognize the signs and symptoms within themselves, or if they do, may be resistant to come forward for fear of reprisal or the stigma of being seen as weak or unable to do their job. It is imperative that if your employer recognizes signs and symptoms or if you recognize them within yourself that you seek appropriate support and resources. Do not leave it unchecked.

If your employer does not have available resources or does not allow you to access them without judgement, you must advocate for yourself in order to obtain the appropriate support. Any issues should be dealt with effectively, constructively and confidentially.

In order to mitigate risk factors related to burnout and vicarious trauma, personal and organizational protective factors must be in place. Remember, however, that these protective factors, although helpful and may mitigate risk, do not make you immune to experiencing burnout or vicarious trauma within your job. It is important to know that you are not alone, seek help, seek support and know that you are not the only one struggling with similar issues.

Self care and self reflection cannot be stressed enough when working in the child and youth care field. We will cover self care in more detail in Chapter 12.

Self Reflection

Self reflection is a common practice that you will frequently use within your CYC practice. Self reflection is invaluable when it come to trauma.

Self reflection involves stepping back from your daily work and analyzing your experiences to come up with different ways of understanding, and to encourage new solutions, strategies and approaches.

Reflective practice is recommended for regular use by staff in the workplace but it can also be a helpful tool for your clients. The goal of reflective practice is to foster growth and development and increase your level of self awareness.

The growth of experiential learning and reflective practice benefits the practitioner and the client by reducing staff burnout, creating better client outcomes, enhancing feelings of support, building greater confidence in one's own ability, improving openness to reviewing their own work, fostering more positive working relationships and client engagement, creating wider pools of ideas, resources and strategies.

In order to practice self reflection, there are some critical skills that are required to be successful:

> **Self-awareness** – Reflect on your thoughts, feelings and actions in relation to your work and consider how a situation has affected you.
>
> **Self-knowledge** – Recognize who you are and how you were shaped by your experiences.
>
> **Critical Analysis** – Consider a situation, identify existing knowledge, challenge assumptions and explore alternatives.
>
> **Synthesis** – Integrate new knowledge, problem solve and predict the likely consequences of actions.
>
> **Evaluation** – What have you learned about yourself through this process? Does this knowledge help you better understand your experience? Has this knowledge helped you explain or solve problems?

In order to positively support self reflection, is it also important to have reflective supervision with your manager or supervisor.

Reflective Supervision

Reflective supervision promotes "learning, growth, engagement, problem identification and resolution" (p.29). In order for reflective supervision to be effective, supervisors need to create an environment based upon the following characteristics.

- Trust
- Safety
- Respect
- Thinking and Feelings
- Collaboration
- Empathic
- Strengths and Resilience
- Nonjudgmental

The National Resource Center for Family Centered Practice (2009) identifies the following skills and barriers in utilizing reflective practice:

Reflective skills include:

- Open ended questions
- Active Listening
- Reframing

- Summarizing
- Metaphors
- Modeling
- Stories
- Use of silence
- Hypothesis building

Barriers to the use of Reflective Practice include:

- Lack of time
- Looking for the perfect question or perfect answer
- Transference/countertransference
- Feelings of being judged
- Lack of trust in helping relationship
- Taking on responsibility for others feelings
- Lack of trust in reflective process
- Need to be in control
- Inconsistency in use of reflective practice
- Over-processing

Other forms of reflective practice include Reflections ON Action, Reflection IN Action and Reflections FOR Action.

Reflections ON Action

Reflections ON Action is used when something has already taken place and the series of questions reflect that. Essentially you are reflecting ON the action you took (Schon, 1983; Brown, Fry and Marshall, 1999).

This process can include:

- Hypothesizing
- Analyzing
- Reviewing
- Proposing alternatives impacts
- Focusing on something possibly missed

Reflections IN Action

Reflections IN Action focuses on client interaction and are most useful when you are "unsure of what might be happening or why it is happening" (p.30).

This process can include discussions surrounding:

- Affect
- Hypothesizing
- Goals/purpose
- Strategies/tools/actions/skills

Reflections FOR Action

These are essentially planning reflections and are focused on preparing for an upcoming contact with a client. Question categories to consider are:

Reflections FOR Action are used for planning and focus on preparation for an upcoming meeting or client contact.

This process includes questions surrounding:

- Goal setting
- Strategies to use
- Hypothesizing
- Identifying potential challenges or barriers and examining ways to address them

Three areas of reflection that are consistent through IN action, FOR action or ON action are:

- **Actions**
- **Thoughts/values/beliefs**
- **Feelings**

Below you will find some examples of questions for each category that will help with your reflective practice which in turn will assist with the response, reaction and management of burnout and/or vicarious trauma.

As a CYC practitioner how will you ensure that you stay balanced in your practice and ensure you have appropriate therapeutic relationships with your clients?

Action Questions

How well did the goals fit what the client/patient needs?

What did you do that made the client/patient feel more engaged?

What could you have done to make the client/patient feel more engaged?

What would have been another way to help the client/patient understand what you were saying?

Thoughts, Values and Belief Questions

Do you believe that the client/patient can achieve the goals that have been set?

Do you trust what the client/patient is saying?

Does your client/patient trust you or the organization? How do you know?

What belief(s) might be preventing the client/patient from moving forward?

What are your belief(s) about pregnancy or parenting that may impact your work with clients/patients?

> **Feeling Questions**
>
> Can you identify a feeling or feelings you had when working with a particular client/patient?
>
> What was happening to stimulate that feeling? What was being said or done?
>
> Were you able to identify what the client/patient was feeling? What other feelings might have been involved?
>
> How transparent was the client/patient or you in expressing or showing your feelings?
>
> How might your feeling be of benefit?
>
> How might your feeling be a barrier or hindrance?

Understanding the categories of impact: burnout, vicarious trauma and secondary trauma is a very important skill to carry with you throughout your career.

Understanding the process, consequences, risk and protective factors are also important and essential skills to carry throughout your career.

No one is immune to burnout or vicarious trauma, and sadly, it is very common in our field of choice, however, being prepared, knowing the risk factors, signs and symptoms can be helpful and useful resources in navigating and facilitating support and resources.

Along with your skills, education, knowledge, self reflection, the ability to self advocate, a supportive workplace, and a network of resources, you will be able to successfully manage whatever comes your way!

Chapter 11 - Let's Reflect

Describe a time when you have experienced burnout, vicarious trauma or secondary trauma. How did you deal with it? what supports did you seek out? How was it resolved?

Chapter 11 – Worksheet

1. Write down 5 words that you think of when you hear burnout.

2. Write down 5 words that you think of when you hear vicarious trauma.

3. Have you experienced any burnout, vicarious trauma symptoms?

5. Have you noticed a colleague, friend or relative that has experienced burnout or vicarious trauma?

6. What are your risk factors under each of these categories?
   - Personal
   - Work
   - Community

7. Which individual protective factors are present in your life?

8. Which organizational protective factors are present in your work life?

Chapter 11 Checklist

I understand and can define/apply the following:

- ☐ Burnout
- ☐ Vicarious trauma
- ☐ Individual Risk factors
- ☐ Work risk factors
- ☐ Community risk factors
- ☐ Personality and coping style
- ☐ Current life circumstances
- ☐ Social Supports
- ☐ Spiritual connections and resources
- ☐ Work Style
- ☐ Role at work
- ☐ Work setting and exposure to trauma
- ☐ Environmental Conditions
- ☐ Agency and supervisory support
- ☐ Culture
- ☐ Community Resources
- ☐ Protective Factors
- ☐ Organizational Protective Factors
- ☐ Self Reflection
- ☐ Self-awareness
- ☐ Synthesis
- ☐ Evaluation
- ☐ Reflection on Action
- ☐ Reflection in Action
- ☐ Reflection for Action
- ☐ Action Questions
- ☐ Thoughts, Values and Belief Questions
- ☐ Feeling Questions

References and Resources

Brown, M., Fry, H. & Marshall, S. (1999). Reflective Practice. In H Fry, S Ketteridge & S Marshall (Eds.), A handbook for teaching and learning in higher education: enhancing academic practice. London: Kogan Page.

National Resource Center for Family Centered Practice (2009). Committed to Excellence Through Supervision, Module III, p. 14 (USDHHS Grant #90CT0111). The University of Iowa School of Social Work.

Schon, D. (1983). The reflective practitioner. New York: Basic Books.

Chapter 12: How do I Balance Education, Work and Personal Life?

> **Real Life Story**
>
> While at a conference I was chatting with a fellow attendee. She was sharing her day timer with me. It was a work of art – colour coded, tabbed, labelled with stickers, and so on. I was very impressed. I also noted that every day she had blocked out an hour of her day. This time slot was labelled as "ME."
>
> I asked her about this ongoing appointment with herself. She said she was not making time to balance her life and the first thing to go by the wayside was self-care. So from that time on, she would schedule "ME" time. She would not schedule anything during this time and if asked, she responded that she already had an appointment booked. She would use this hour to do something she enjoyed, read a book, go to the gym, take a walk, or daydream. She would do something specifically that made her happy.
>
> She was very protective of her ME time and found that she began leading a much happier, well-balanced life because of the commitment she made to herself.

According to Statistics Canada (2018), the total number of students enrolled in Canadian universities and colleges from 2015 to 2016 was 2,034,957.

The most popular programs include business, management and public administration, humanities, social and behavioural sciences, and law.

This is a significant amount of people enrolled in post-secondary programs who are hoping to enter the work force in their field of study. However, until that happens, how do they all cope with managing everyday stressors such as money, time management and self care? All of which are important for a successful post-secondary experience.

Your chosen career as a Child and Youth Care Practitioner is a very brave and bold choice. You will find yourself facing situations that you never thought possible and you will feel defeat and joy at extreme levels. You will work countless hours and help innumerable children, youth and families.

You will be pursuing a career that requires a commitment to lifelong learning, education and self-care. It is easy to get discouraged when you have so much on your plate along with the everyday life stressors.

This Chapter will provide you with some tips and tricks for life balance, time management and self-care.

EDUCATION

You are likely enrolled in a 3 year Child and Youth Care program with a full course load including placement either currently or in the upcoming semesters.

Although it may seem overwhelming at first, having an organized system will help you stay on track and ensure that you meet due dates, expectations and requirements.

Attending class is pivotal for success in the CYC field. Your teachers will impart their wisdom and experience upon you and that will form the foundation of your practice. You will take all the tools they provide you with and build your practice using your own personality and skills that you develop along the way.

It is during class time that you will learn the basics of child and youth care, along with all the other subjects you will be required to take. During class time, as you know, you will have the opportunity to discuss, share and present information amongst your fellow classmates. This will allow you a glimpse into their practices, skills and fundamental beliefs.

John McClung (2015) suggest that there are techniques for maintaining a balance in your life. His list of tips include:

1. Create a schedule and update it

Make use of the app on your phone, buy a day planner or use a desktop calendar. Whatever helps keep you organized the best is the right format for you. Make sure you take the time to add your work, class and social schedules and update them on a regular basis.

Ensure that you also factor in time to complete your homework and other chores.

2. Work ahead and avoid procrastinating

It is very easy to fall into the pattern of leaving things until the very last minute, however, this allows your work to grow with uncompleted tasks. It is harder to stay motivated when you feel overwhelmed. Getting, and staying ahead of assignments, readings and papers will reduce the amount of work that piles up hence reducing the feelings of stressed and being overwhelmed. Working ahead, or avoiding procrastination also allows you to enjoy more social and/or personal time to do the things you enjoy.

3. Prioritize

Organizing your work in a way that works for you will allow you to be on top of all your due dates and assignments. If you prioritize them based on the due date you will be assured that you work is handed in on time. Be sure to review the course syllabus to determine exact due dates as well as the value of each assignment/paper/presentation. A paper with a high value, will likely have more expectations than a small discussion or post.

Erin Pettus (2021) adds the following tips to balance your school and work life:

4. Use your support network

Your support network is usually made up of people who are in a position to help you attain your goals. It may include family, friends, classmates, professors etc.

You will notice that you will likely be placed in a cohort, or block of students in your program and you will stay together for the duration of your diploma. These individuals can act as a strong support system as they are participating in the same classes and experiences as you are.

Your family may be able to support you by assisting with taking on more domestic tasks to free up your time to focus on academics.

5. Manage your time

Time management can be can difficult task for many due to competing priorities and commitments. Try to prioritize your tasks based on their level of importance. Ensure that you are aware of deadlines and due dates, but also ensure that you are making time to practice self-care

6. Plan Your tasks

Use your time efficiently and plan ahead. Identify commonalities in your work and combine or streamline your activities to reduce redundancies.

7. Pick courses that interest you

Choose to study something that you enjoy. This will keep you motivated and interested while you learn and complete your assignments.

WORK

While attending a full time College level program you may also be working part time or considering working part time. This can be for various reasons but the most common is to allow you to be able to afford the cost of post-secondary education. You also may be working part time in your field of study and wish to continue to do so with the hopes of gaining valuable, relevant experience that will possibly lead to full time employment upon graduation.

The benefits of working while you earn your diploma include earning money and mastering important soft skills required for your career. It is a challenge to study and work. Throughout this process you will gain experience with saving money and hopefully graduating with less debt. You will learn to manage your time, and make new professional connections.

The disadvantages of working while earning a diploma is that it can affect your grades. You will have less free time for extracurricular activities which is important for your life-balance.

Educational institutions understand that they will need to support their students. It is important for you to explore all the services and options available at your school to help you manage and balance all of your responsibilities.

Your employer will also understand that you need support. Make sure that your employer is aware of your studies. Talk to your boss. And, outside of work, talk to your family and friends. Utilize all of your social networks to help you succeed.

You will need to be aware of signs of stress and when challenges become too overwhelming. Monitor your health and emotions. Be aware of anxiety, problems sleeping, irritability, depression, addiction, and changes in your health and mental wellness.

Remember to make time for yourself, to relax, reflect, exercise, connect with friends and family, walk your dog, garden, and treat yourself.

In addition, you can relieve stress by exercising, laughing, asking for help, talking with others, being optimistic.

Watch for signs of burn-out. If you are feeling emotional, physical, and mental exhaustion, you may be experiencing burnout. Burnout affects your productivity, drains your energy, and as mentioned, affects your health and mental wellness. Burnout can spill over into other areas of your life, your work, studies, and family and social life. This process can be gradual and can go unnoticed until it reaches a critical point. As such, it is important to regularly check-in with yourself and reflect on your emotional and physical health.

The Difference Between Stress and Burnout

According to Smith, Segal, Ph.D., and Robinson (2020), burnout "may be the result of unrelenting stress, but it isn't the same as too much stress." Stress "involves too many pressures that demand too much of you physically and mentally." Burnout is not enough: feeling empty and mentally exhausted, devoid of motivation, and beyond caring." For instance, stress can be characterized by over-engagement and burnout by disengagement. Emotions can be overactive vs. blunted; hyperactivity vs. hopelessness; and anxiety vs depression.

Smith, Segal, Ph.D., and Robinson (2020), identify the "Three R" approach to deal with burnout:

1. Recognize – Watch for the warning signs of burnout
2. Reverse – Undo the damage by seeking support and managing stress
3. Resilience – Build your resilience to stress by taking care of your physical and emotional health

Sometime, people need to change their circumstances, environment and context in order to deal with burnout. First, remember why you decided to study and work and take on challenges in your life. This can help you to refocus and reflect upon what motivates you. '

You can also turn to other people for advice, meet new people, join new clubs and do different activities. Ultimately, you can seek professional help.

Self Care

Self-care is an essential CYC skill. Self-care refers to activities that you practice in order to stay healthy and well while working in a stressful field of employment.

There are many dimensions of wellness that relate to self-care, at any time, if one or more are not attended to, you can feel like something is lacking in your self-care routine.

The dimensions of wellness include:
- Physical
- Emotional/psychological
- Spiritual
- Social
- Environmental

Harmony in all these areas can contribute to your self-care.

As a CYC you will likely work long hours that include varying shifts. This can be very taxing, especially if you are also taking courses, taking care of a family and trying to take care of yourself. You will also be exposed to a great deal of trauma as well as completing physically and emotionally demanding tasks.

When creating a self-care plan, start by looking at the dimensions of wellness listed above to help you target the areas that may be lacking attention. Try to find activities or make plans that satisfy each of the areas.

For example:

Physical: It is often difficult to incorporate physical activity when we are working long hours and various shifts. You will feel tired and not necessarily want to engage in any physical activity regardless of how strenuous or moderate it may be. Our jobs as CYC Practitioners can be physically demanding and draining, which can lead us to want to rest during our time off. We also know that physical activity can alleviate stress and is healthy for our hearts and bodies.

To meet this dimension for your self-care plan you may choose to go for walks, take a run, ride a bike or go for a swim. These activities will allow you time for yourself as well as assist with your overall health and wellness.

Emotional and psychological: As a CYC you will be dealing with a great deal of trauma and it is often difficult to leave those issues "at the office."

Your mental health is as important, if not more important, than any of the other dimensions. Your emotional well being is pivotal to you being a compassionate, caring, successful CYC Practitioner. We always seem to take care of our physical health, for instance, we go to the doctor if we have pain or are sick, and we go to the optometrist for our eyes. However, we often unconsciously neglect our mental health.

As part of your self-care plan you should reflect upon this area and ensure that you have a supportive outlet for your emotional and psychological health such as a peer, a trusted family member, work colleague or a psychologist or psychiatrist.

While it is important to maintain confidentiality when addressing this area, you will need to discuss how you are feeling and debrief with someone you trust.

Spiritual: Spiritual self-care does not just mean religion, although that is often where our minds go when we read the word. It definitely can mean religion, and many people find great peace and harmony in their religious practices. Research has shown that those who practice regular spirituality, be it religious or otherwise, show lower signs of stress and are able to manage stressful situations more positively.

Spirituality can also mean finding peaceful and reflective states of mind or moments when you can relax and recharge. These states or moments can be when you listen to music, do yoga or meditate, go for a walk or paint. These activities are usually a time for quiet reflection and personal rejuvenation.

If you do not already practice any type of spirituality, this may take practice and focus, however, this process in itself can be rewarding.

Social: Socializing is also a very big part of self-care. We can often get caught up in our jobs and responsibilities and we begin focusing on them all the time, even when we are not in the workplace. This can be exhausting, and it interferes with our ability to practice positive self-care. Being social is a very big part of self-care. Maintain social contacts allow us the opportunity to have fun, enjoy ourselves, relax and spend time with loved ones.

We can forget about work for a while and be with people whose company we enjoy. Go for a manicure, take a walk with a friend, have lunch with a buddy. I am sure you all know how fulfilling it can be to spend time with friends and family to re-charge and relax.

Environmental: Environmental wellness can mean many things, but in the context of self-care I will be referring to your immediate surroundings. Having a clean, organized space in which to live allows you to feel uncluttered and focused. This alone can be relaxing.

We do not often think about how our environment impacts our well being. If your workspace, home, bedroom or living space is cluttered, dirty, chaotic, or not functioning optimally this can impact how you function at home and in the workplace.

It is important to maintain a clean and organized work area, not only for your own well-being, but for your colleagues who will enter the shift after you.

Maintaining a clean and organized home area can also contribute to feelings of calm and peacefulness. I am certain that all of you do not make your beds everyday; however, think of the days when your bed is made and your room is clean, your laundry is done and put away and your surfaces are clean and uncluttered. Try to practice this daily so that your surroundings become a place of peace, not one of chaos. After cleaning and organizing your space reflect on how this makes you feel. Do you feel calm satisfied?

After reviewing the self-care areas listed above, start to formulate a self-care plan. This plan will be a living document that you can alter, adjust, add and subtract from as your circumstances or your interests change. Nothing in your self-care plan is carved in stone, it is suggested to be a guide for you to ensure that you are taking care of yourself and taking time for yourself.

Keep in mind that if you are already doing activities to fulfill certain areas of self-care, continue to do those activities. This plan is about doing what you are not doing or changing what you are doing that is not making you happy. This is about setting personal boundaries between your work and yourself.

Use the chart below to start your self-care plan. Try to think of 3 activities or practices for each of the wellness dimensions.

When completing your plan think of short- and long-term self-care goals that you would like to achieve, and how you will attain them. Include in your activities the 5 "w's":

- who will participate, yourself or with others?
- what activity will you do for this dimension?
- why did you choose this activity or practice?
- when will you participate in this activity (how often, for how long)?
- where will you participate in this activity?

Make sure to revisit your plan regularly to ensure it is meeting your needs as well as working within your available time and schedules. If you find something is not working then change it, but don't give up. We cannot stress enough how important self-care is in the CYC field, and it is up to you to ensure that you are meeting your needs. You've got this!

	Activity 1	Activity 2	Activity 3
Physical			
Emotional/Psychological			
Spiritual			
Social			
Environmental			
Short-term goal			
Long-term goal			

Chapter 12 - Let's Reflect

How are you currently meeting the need for work, life, school balance?

Discuss any changes you feel need to be made to your current plan.

Chapter 12 – Worksheet

1. Explain what work/life/school balance means?

2. List 3 things to help you achieve success at school.

3. List 3 things that would help you achieve success at work.

4. List 3 things that will help you achieve social success.

5. Define burnout.

6. Discuss the differences between burnout and stress.

7. List 3 signs of:
   - Physical burnout

   - Emotional burnout

8. List 5 things that contribute to self-care.

Chapter 12 – Checklist

- ☐ I understand the need for self-care

- ☐ I understand the ways to balance work/life/school

- ☐ I understand that stress and burnout are not the same

- ☐ I understand the signs and symptoms of burnout

- ☐ I have a plan to manage school/work/life balance

- ☐ I practice self-care

References and Resources

Johns Hopkins University. (2021). School-life balance. Retrieved from https://jhsap.org/self_help_resources/school-life_balance/

Smith, M., Segal, J., and Robinson, L., (2020). Burnout Prevention and Treatment. Retrieved from https://www.helpguide.org/articles/stress/burnout-prevention-and-recovery.htm

McClung, J. (2015). 5 ways to maintain balance betwen work, school, and life. Retrieved from https://www.wayup.com/guide/community/5-ways-to-maintain-balance-between-work-school-and-life/

Pettus, E. (2021). 7 tips to help you balance school and work. Retrieved from https://abound.college/finishcollege/advice/7-tips-to-help-you-balance-school-and-work/

Statistics Canada. (2018). Post secondary enrolments. Retrieved from https://www.statcan.gc.ca/eng/dai/smr08/2018/smr08_220_2018#a6

The College of St. Scholastica. (2018). Working while in college: Weighing the pros & cons. Retrieved from http://www.css.edu/the-sentinel-blog/working-while-in-college-weighing-the-pros-and-cons.html

CPSIA information can be obtained
at www.ICGtesting.com
Printed in the USA
BVHW060835290521
608141BV00004BA/21